Great People of the
BIBLE

saint mary's press

The Subcommittee on the Catechism, United States Conference of Catholic Bishops, has found this catechetical text, copyright 2010, to be in conformity with the *Catechism of the Catholic Church*.

Nihil Obstat: Rev. Andrew J. Beerman, STL
               Censor Librorum
               March 25, 2009
Imprimatur: †Most Rev. Bernard J. Harrington, DD
               Bishop of Winona
               March 25, 2009

The nihil obstat and imprimatur are official declarations that a book or pamphlet is free of doctrinal or moral error. No implication is contained therein that those who have granted the nihil obstat or imprimatur agree with the contents, opinions, or statements expressed, nor do they assume any legal responsibility associated with publication.

The publishing team included Brian Singer-Towns, development editor; Lorraine Kilmartin, reviewer; prepress and manufacturing coordinated by the production departments of Saint Mary's Press.

The background pages were revised by Lee Danesco from original content supplied by Therese Brown, Rick Keller-Scholz, Christine Schmertz Navarro, Ann Nunes, Jeannie Pomanowski, Brian Singer-Towns, and Chris Wardwell. The activity pages were created and designed by Gabriel Publications.

Illustrations by Pernsteiner Creative Group

Printed in the United States of America

2303

ISBN 978-0-88489-690-6

CONTENTS

The Bible: God's Word for Us!

"For God loved the world so much that he gave his only Son, so that everyone who believes in him may not die but have eternal life."

(John 3:16)

There is probably no better way to sum up the message of the Bible than this one verse from the Gospel of John. The Bible is the story of God's love for the world, right from the first moment of creation. We human beings sin against God and each other, turning away from God's love. Yet, we cannot prevent God's loving plan from being fulfilled—thanks be to God!

God is greater than anything we could possibly understand or know by ourselves. We only know God because he chooses to show—or to reveal—himself to us. In the Bible God reveals himself and his plan for us in a way no other book can do. That is because God is the author of the Bible. Not that God actually wrote the words down, but the Holy Spirit inspired the human authors to write down what God wanted us to know. Because of this, we can count on the Bible to be absolutely true, without any error, when it teaches what God wants us to know to spend eternal life with him.

Why is the Bible so big? It is big because God is so big! Throughout all history God has been revealing himself to the human race. He has done so through creation, miraculous signs, and the words of the prophets. But God does more than just reveal himself through words and signs. He gave himself to us through the life, death, and Resurrection of his Son, Jesus Christ. It takes many words to tell all these stories of God's ongoing relationship with the people he created.

Studying the Bible takes time. You could spend your whole lifetime studying it and praying with it (which many Christians do!). Even so, you always find new insights and new ways to apply it to your life. That is because the Holy Spirit is at work within us, helping us understand God's Word. With the Holy Spirit's help, you can always understand more about what God is revealing through the human authors who wrote the Bible.

You are not too young to start reading the Bible. A good place to start is by studying some of the holy and heroic people of the Bible. Be inspired by how they responded to God and how God worked through them. You might be surprised to find out they weren't all perfect people. They struggled with sin and temptation just as you do. But they became great and virtuous people because they realized their need for God. In the end they were willing to trust God and let him work through them.

This textbook and its activities will help you become familiar with some of the greatest people of the Bible: good and holy people who loved and followed God. All you need to work through its activities is a Bible, a curious mind, and an open heart. Most of all, as you learn about these Bible people, keep asking yourself this: "What is God teaching me through this person's life?" Always remember that God loves you and wants to share himself with you through the Bible, his holy Word.

> **"All Scripture is inspired by God and is useful for teaching the truth, rebuking error, correcting faults, and giving instruction for right living."**
>
> **(2 Timothy 3:16)**

The Scriptures and Tradition

God wants us to know him. So throughout history God has revealed himself to human beings. We call this activity Revelation. God's most complete Revelation was through the person of his Son, Jesus Christ. Inspired by the Holy Spirit, the Apostles handed on to others—in words and writing—what they had learned from their time with Jesus. They passed on everything our loving God revealed to save us from sin and death. The successors of the Apostles, the Pope and bishops of the Church, continue to pass on this Revelation without error for all ages until Christ returns in glory.

God's Revelation is handed on in a special way through the Bible—in both the Old and New Testaments. It is also handed on through something called Tradition. This word actually means "handing on." Tradition helps us better understand the Scriptures (another word for the Bible), and the Scriptures help us better understand what God reveals through Tradition. Together the Scriptures and Tradition form a single Deposit of Faith. We must accept and honor both equally to learn all God wants to reveal to us.

With the Holy Spirit guiding her, the Church draws upon the Scriptures and Tradition to hand on the faith to each new generation. Through the liturgy, through Catholic teachings and doctrines, and through our lives together, God's Revelation continually informs us and is our guiding light.

In the Bible, God shows—or reveals—himself to us. We learn about his love for all humanity. God's words and deeds in the Bible help us understand his plan to save us from sin and death and bring us to eternal life. Because of this activity, the history told in the Bible is sometimes called salvation history. Following is a brief overview of salvation history.

Primeval History. The Bible begins with stories—filled with symbolism about how God created everything that exists. The stories of Adam and Eve, Cain and Abel, Noah and the flood, and the tower of Babel teach us that God created everything. They also show us that human beings have a special place in creation. The stories teach us that sin destroys our relationships with God and one another.

Patriarchs. In this period of salvation history, God begins to form a special relationship with a chosen group of people. He makes a special promise, called a covenant, with a man named Abraham. God promises that Abraham and his wife, Sarah, will have a son in their old age. God promises that their descendants will be numerous. He promises that they will inherit a Promised Land.

Egypt and the Exodus. The descendants of Abraham—now called Israelites—are in slavery in Egypt. God hears their cries and calls Moses to lead the people out of slavery. The Israelites' escape from Egypt and journey to the Promised Land is called the Exodus. On the way to the Promised Land, the Israelites stop at Mount Sinai. There, God extends to all the Israelites the Covenant he made with Abraham. He gives Moses Ten Commandments, which the people must obey as part of their Covenant promises.

Settling the Promised Land. Moses dies. God calls a new leader, Joshua. He will lead the people into the Promised Land, which other people inhabit. The Israelites must fight to gain control of the land. When they trust God, they are successful in their battles. When they do not trust God, they fail. Eventually they gain control of the land. Each of the twelve Tribes is given its own section of the land.

Kingdoms of Judah and Israel. When the Israelites want their own king, God reluctantly agrees to their plea. He has Samuel anoint Saul as the first king of Israel. David follows Saul as the next king. David is a mighty warrior who unites all the twelve Tribes into one kingdom called Israel. David's son Solomon becomes the third king of the Israelites. He builds a Temple at Jerusalem, the capital city. After Solomon's death there is disagreement among the tribes. The kingdom splits in two. The northern ten tribes form Israel. The southern two form Judah. During this time God calls prophets to remind the kings and the people to obey their Covenant with God.

Exile and Return. Despite the prophets' warnings, the people of Israel and Judah continue to turn away from God's Covenant with them. So God lets their kingdoms be conquered. Many of the people are taken into captivity outside their homeland. This time is called the Exile. Prophets like Ezekiel comfort the Israelites with the promise that God is still with them. Fifty years pass in exile. Then a new king, Cyrus of Persia, comes to rule over the kingdom that captured the Israelites. He allows the people—now called Judeans, or Jews—to return to Jerusalem to rebuild it and the Temple.

Life of Jesus Christ. When the time is right, God sends his only Son, Jesus Christ, into the world. When Jesus is born, the Romans rule Israel. Some of the Jews hope for a mighty warrior and king like David. They hope he will drive out the Romans. Jesus shows a different way. He preaches love, justice, and forgiveness. When Jesus is killed, his followers think all is lost. Instead, after three days God raises Jesus from the dead. God's saving plan is now fulfilled.

Early Christian Church. After his Resurrection, Jesus instructs his closest followers, the Apostles, to go and spread the Good News of salvation to all people. The Holy Spirit gives them the courage to tell others about Jesus Christ. Sometimes people who do not believe in Jesus persecute and kill the Apostles. People like Peter and Paul spread the message to other cities and regions. Soon Christianity spreads throughout the Roman Empire.

Some Heroic Bible People

Primeval History
- Adam and Eve
- Noah

Patriarchs
- Abraham and Sarah

Egypt and the Exodus
- Moses, Miriam, and Aaron

Settling the Promised Land
- Joshua
- Samson
- Ruth

Kingdoms of Judah and Israel
- King David
- King Solomon
- Isaiah

Exile and Return
- Ezekiel
- Ezra and Nehemiah
- The Maccabees

Life of Jesus Christ
- Mary of Nazareth
- John the Baptist
- Jesus, the Christ
- Peter
- Mary Magdalene

Early Christian Church
- Paul
- Priscilla and Aquila

SALVATION HISTORY

History told from the perspective of God's breaking through is called salvation history. This time line gives a big-picture view of salvation history. In the spaces below, create your own big picture of salvation history with a drawing representing an event that occurred during each time period. Write a brief caption for each drawing.

PRIMEVAL HISTORY **CREATION–2000 BC**	**PATRIARCHS** **2000 BC–1700 BC**
EGYPT AND THE EXODUS **1700 BC–1250 BC**	**SETTLING THE PROMISED LAND** **1250 BC–1050 BC**
KINGDOMS OF JUDAH AND ISRAEL **1050 BC–587 BC**	**EXILE AND RETURN** **587 BC–AD 1**
LIFE OF JESUS CHRIST **AD 1–AD 33**	**EARLY CHRISTIAN CHURCH** **AD 33–AD 100**

The Bible is divided into two major sections, the Old Testament and the New Testament. Catholic bibles have forty-six books in the Old Testament that we accept as sacred and inspired by God. The bibles most Protestants use have thirty-nine books in the Old Testament. That is the main difference between Catholic and Protestant bibles.

The Old Testament books include many different kinds of writings. You will find history, poetry, legends, laws, wise sayings, short stories, and the words of prophets. The Old Testament books are mainly about God's special relationship with his Chosen People. At different times these people are called Hebrews, Israelites, Judeans, and Jews. During their history God breaks through and calls the Chosen People to recognize him as their one and only God. God promises to bless them in a special way. He asks the Chosen People to be faithful in following his commands.

The holy promises between God and the Chosen People are called covenants. These are solemn agreements in which all involved agree to keep their commitments forever. *Testament* is another word for *covenant,* so the Old Testament is the story of the Covenant between God and his Chosen People—who eventually become the Jewish people. For this reason, most of the books of the Old Testament are also the Jewish people's sacred Scriptures. So the Old Testament isn't "old" because it is out of date. It is "old" because it is the story of how God first made his Covenant with his Chosen People.

To fully understand God's plan for the human race, we need both the Old and the New Testaments. In the Old Testament, God reveals the love he has for us. The stories teach us how sin keeps us from being in a completely loving relationship with God. The Old Testament shows how, through holy and courageous people, God breaks through to put his Chosen People on the right path. The stories in the Old Testament prepare us to understand how Jesus Christ fulfills God's Covenant to save us from sin and death.

Reflection

Page through the Old Testament of your Bible. What stories do you recognize? If you have any favorite stories in the Old Testament, what are they? What do they teach you about God?

Sections of the Old Testament

The Old Testament in Christian bibles is usually divided into four different sections. Here is some information on each section:

The Pentateuch or Torah. These first five biblical books are the heart of the Old Testament. They contain the stories of Creation and stories about how sin entered the world. They tell how God broke through to first make his Covenant with Noah and Abraham. The Book of Exodus tells how God led his people out of slavery through the leadership of Moses. At Mount Sinai, God extended the Covenant to all his Chosen People and gave them the Ten Commandments.

The Historical Books. These sixteen books are mostly religious history and some short novels. They tell how the Chosen People settled in the Promised Land. Eventually they became a kingdom led by kings like Saul, David, and Solomon. But the rulers and the people often worshiped false gods and ignored the poor. So God sent prophets like Elijah and Elisha to call the people to be faithful to the Covenant. The historical books also have stories about heroes like Ruth, Tobit, Judith, and Esther.

The Wisdom Books. These seven books contain the collected wisdom of the Chosen People. They include the songs the people used in worship and prayer. They contain advice for living good and holy lives. The Song of Songs has poetry about the goodness of sexuality. The Book of Job is a debate about why good people suffer bad things.

The Books of the Prophets. These eighteen books contain the messages of important prophets. The prophets delivered God's message to the Chosen People. They warned the Chosen People against worshiping false gods. They challenged the Chosen People to act fairly and care for the poor. The prophets also offered comfort and hope when the people thought God had abandoned them. Some prophets promised a future Savior, the Messiah, who would bring God's love, justice, and peace to the world.

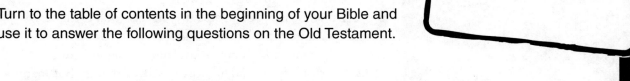

Turn to the table of contents in the beginning of your Bible and use it to answer the following questions on the Old Testament.

1. How many books are in the Old Testament? _____
2. What is the first book of the Old Testament? _____
3. What is the last book of the Old Testament? _____
4. Which book of the Old Testament is the shortest? _____
5. Which book of the Old Testament is the longest? _____
6. What are the four sections of the Old Testament? _____

_____

_____

_____

7. List the five books of the Pentateuch. _____

_____

_____

_____

_____

8. Which book comes after Psalms? _____
9. In which section do you find each of the following books?

1 Kings_____   Nahum_____

Song of Songs_____   Jonah_____

Now try looking up some Bible passages. Look up each passage below and write the word indicated to complete a sentence about the Old Testament.

10. Exodus 12:37 Write the second word of the passage in the space before the (10).

11. Judges 10:14 Write the tenth word of the passage in the space before the (11).

12. Isaiah 32:18 Write the second word of the passage in the space before the (12).

The Old Testament is the story of the

_____(10),

God's _____(11)

_____(12).

God's plan for our salvation begins with the first human beings, Adam and Eve. In the Book of Genesis, we find two parts to their story. First, God creates Adam. His name in Hebrew means "human being." God forms him from the earth and breathes life into him. But man is not meant to be alone, so God also creates a woman from Adam's flesh so Adam will have a companion just like him. The woman's name, Eve, means "living." God puts Adam and Eve in the Garden of Eden. There they have everything they need to be happy. In the garden God speaks to Adam and Eve face to face. There they live in peaceful friendship with God, each other, and all of creation.

Unfortunately, the story of Adam and Eve does not end with them living in the garden forever. In the second part of the story, a tricky snake (who the Bible later reveals to be Satan; see Revelation 12:9) persuades them that what God has given them is not enough. He says that if they eat the fruit of a tree God has placed off limits, they will become just like God. Adam and Eve have a decision to make. They choose not to trust God. Instead they give in to the snake's temptation and eat the forbidden fruit.

This first disobedience is called Original Sin. It is a major turning point in the story of salvation. It causes Adam and Eve and every person after them—except Jesus and his mother, Mary—to lose the original state of holiness God intended for us. We do not live in perfect unity. Instead, we are separated from God, one another, and the rest of creation.

The story of Adam and Eve reveals that we were created to find our happiness by living close to God. But human beings since then have continued to disobey God. God shows his love by not abandoning Adam and Eve or us. God promises that a future descendant of Adam and Eve will defeat the snake's schemes. When the time is right, God sends his Son, Jesus Christ, as a kind of New Adam. God overcomes the damage of Original Sin through the saving work of his Son, Jesus.

Reflection

Imagine you could put Adam and Eve on trial in a courtroom. What questions would you ask about their decision to eat the forbidden fruit? Do you think the serpent shares the blame for the sin of Adam and Eve? Explain.

Bible Passages About Adam and Eve

Genesis 2:4–15
God creates a man, animals, and a woman.
Genesis 3:1–6
Adam and Eve eat from the forbidden fruit tree.
Genesis 3:7–13
Adam and Eve hide from God.
Genesis 3:14–24
God punishes and banishes Adam and Eve.

ADAM AND EVE

Read the story of Adam and Eve in Genesis 2:4—3:24, then fill in the blanks in the statements below. To find out if your answers are correct, find each of your answers in the word search. Put the unused letters from the word search in the spaces at the bottom of the page to spell out a fact about Adam and Eve.

1. When the Lord God created the earth, nothing was growing on it because there was no __ __ __ __ and no man to cultivate the ground.
2. The Lord God formed man out of the clay, or soil, of the __ __ __ __ __ __ .
3. The Lord God planted a garden in __ __ __ __ .
4. The tree of __ __ __ __ was planted in the middle of the garden.
5. There was a stream, or river, in the garden that divided into __ __ __ __ branches.
6. The job of the __ __ __ was to cultivate and care for the garden.
7. The man was allowed to eat of any tree except the tree of the knowledge of __ __ __ __ and bad.
8. The man gave names to all the __ __ __ __ __ __ __ .
9. The woman was made from one of the __ __ __ __ of the man.
10. The snake tempted the woman to eat the __ __ __ __ __ .
11. The man and the woman realized that they were naked and sewed together some __ __ __ __ __ __ __ __ __ . (TWO WORDS)
12. They hid among some __ __ __ __ __ when they heard the Lord God in the garden.
13. The man named his wife Eve because she was the __ __ __ __ __ __ of all human beings.
14. The __ __ __ __ __ __ __ made clothes from animal skins for them. (TWO WORDS)
15. The Lord God sent the man and the woman out of the garden and placed a flaming __ __ __ __ __ outside it to guard the tree of life.

A	D	A	L	O	R	D	G	O	D
A	D	N	M	A	F	R	N	D	G
D	R	I	E	V	I	E	D	O	N
N	O	M	S	B	G	I	O	I	E
U	W	A	S	E	L	D	A	R	F
O	S	L	S	O	E	R	B	U	I
R	E	S	Y	E	A	R	D	O	L
G	N	E	D	E	V	G	T	F	M
O	M	O	T	H	E	R	D	+	A
T	I	U	R	F	S	+	+	+	N

__ __ __ __ __ __ __ __ __ __ __

__ __ __ __ __ __ __ __

__ __ __.

Among the many descendants of Adam and Eve is a man named Noah. During Noah's time, most other human beings are living lives filled with sin and evil. But Noah stands out before God as a truly good man.

In the story of Noah, we learn that God has become disappointed with his creatures. He decides to wipe them all out by sending a tremendous Flood to destroy the earth. Noah alone is a good and just man. For that reason God decides to save Noah from the Flood. God instructs Noah to build a large boat, or ark. Then Noah is to bring on board the ark his family and a supply of food. He is also to bring a male and female from every species of animal.

As strange as God's words might sound, Noah does exactly as God commands. Then, just as God foretells, a great Flood arrives, with rains lasting forty days. It destroys every living thing except Noah and those he gathers safely aboard the ark.

When the land becomes dry once more, God tells Noah to leave the ark and return to the land. Once off the boat, Noah builds an altar and offers a sacrifice to God. He wants to thank God for the blessing of life God has given him. Then God makes a Covenant, a sacred promise, with Noah. He promises Noah and all his descendants that never again will a flood destroy the earth and all living creatures.

God places a rainbow in the sky. He promises that the rainbow will be an everlasting sign of the Covenant he makes with Noah. The story and the rainbow are constant reminders that God rewards goodness. He works to save us from the effects of sin.

Reflection

When God prepares to destroy the earth and all living creatures, he decides to save Noah. What do you think is so special about Noah's life that convinces God he is worth saving? Can you think of people today who live like Noah?

Bible Passages About Noah

Genesis 6:5–12
Evil fills the earth.

Genesis 6:13–22
God tells Noah to build a boat.

Genesis 7:1–24
The Flood starts.

Genesis 8:11–19
The Flood ends.

Genesis 8:20—9:17
God makes a Covenant with Noah.

In the story of Noah, God destroys the world because of the evil humans are committing. After reading the story in Genesis 6:5—9:17, complete the crossword below. The numbers in parentheses are chapters and verses in Genesis.

ACROSS

1. God told Noah to build this, which is also called an ark. (6:14)
5. Sign of the covenant, a rain ____. (9:12–13)
7. This occupied people's thoughts and their hearts. (6:5)
8. Number of days Noah had to gather the animals on the ark. (7:1–4)
10. God forbid the taking of ____ life. (9:5–6)
12. He blessed Noah and his sons. (9:1)
14. Mountains on which the ark landed when the waters went down. (8:4)
15. Number of times Noah sent out a dove. (8:8–12)
16. Number of days and nights that it rained. (7:12)

DOWN

2. The dove returned with this kind of leaf. (8:11)
3. God made one with Noah. (9:9)
4. Noah took seven pairs of these kinds of animals. (7:2)
6. Noah's ark was made of this, which is also called timber. (6:14)
8. After Noah and the others had entered the ark, God ____ the door. (7:16)
9. First bird Noah sent out to see if the land was dry. (8:7)
10. Son of Noah. (6:10)
11. When Noah left the ark, he built this to worship God. (8:20)
13. Number of pairs of unclean animals Noah took. (7:2)

Abram and Sarai, as they are originally called, first appear in the Book of Genesis. They are nomads, wanderers who tend their animals in the land of Ur. They respond faithfully to God and his promises. For that reason Abram and Sarai play important parts in God's plan for salvation.

God calls Abram and Sarai to leave their home and move to a faraway land. God promises to give Abram this new land for his own. He promises to make Abram and Sarai the parents of many nations with descendants as numerous as the stars. He further promises that Abram and Sarai's descendants will be a light to all nations.

To Abram and Sarai, God's promise of many descendants seems impossible. They have no children and are already old. Instead of trusting in himself, Abram believes in God and his word. God makes a covenant with Abram to seal his promise. God also changes Abram's name to Abraham. His new name means "father of a multitude." Sarai becomes Sarah.

Abraham and Sarah travel to the land God has promised. Along the way they have many adventures. They also have many opportunities to lose faith in God's promise. But Abraham and Sarah continue to trust in his word.

After twenty-five years of faithful waiting, Sarah gives birth to a son. She and Abraham name him Isaac. It seems their faith has been rewarded.

Soon God tests Abraham's faith again. God tells Abraham to sacrifice Isaac. Abraham does not protest. Instead, with total trust in God, Abraham prepares to give up his son. At the last moment, God stops Abraham. Instead God gives him a sheep to sacrifice.

Abraham and Sarah are great heroes of our faith. Through Sarah, God demonstrates that with him, all things are possible, even childbirth for an elderly woman. Because of his strong faith, Abraham is honored as the father of three great religions: Judaism, Islam, and Christianity.

Reflection

What difficulties would you imagine Abraham and Sarah face when they leave their home for a new land? You face similar challenges when going to a new school, neighborhood, or team. How could you make faith a part of your next move?

Bible Passages About Abraham and Sarah

Genesis 12:1–9
God calls Abram and Sarai to leave Ur.

Genesis 15:1–21
God makes a covenant with Abram.

Genesis 17:1–8
God changes Abram's and Sarai's names.

Genesis 18:1–15
God promises to send Sarah and Abraham a son.

Genesis 21:1–8
Isaac is born.

Genesis 22:1–19
God commands Abraham to sacrifice Isaac.

ABRAHAM AND SARAH

Put the events of Abraham and Sarah's life in the correct order of how they happened. You can figure this out by scanning the headlines in Genesis 11:27—23:20. Number the events 1 through 14 in the space provided. Starting with event number 1, put the bold, underlined letters in the spaces provided at the bottom. Some events have two letters in bold, underlined type. Be sure to put those letters in the spaces in the order in which they appear in the sentence.

(1) _____ Hagar gave birth to A**b**ram's son, Ishma**e**l.

(2) _____ Sarah gav**e** birth to Abraham's son, Isaac.

(3) _____ Abram and Sa**r**ai went to Egypt because there was a fam**i**ne in Canaan.

(4) _____ God changed Abram'**s** name to Abraham and Sarai's name to Sarah and established circumcision as the sign of the covenant.

(5) _____ God promised Sarah and Abraham that they would have a son **i**n their ol**d** age and Sarah laughed.

(6) _____ As a test of faith, God told Ab**r**aham to take his son, Isaac, and offer him up as a **s**acrifice.

(7) _____ A**b**ram and his wife Sarai went with his father, Terah, to Haran.

(8) _____ Abra**h**am bought a piece of land as a burial place for Sarah.

(9) _____ After the defeat of the four kings, Melchizedek brought bread and w**i**ne to Abra**m**.

(10) _____ Abram and Lot parted ways and s**e**parated their belongings.

(11) _____ Abraham and **A**bimelech made a pact at Beer-sheba.

(12) _____ The Lord called Abram to leave his father's ho**u**se in Haran and travel to Canaan with Sarai.

(13) _____ Abram save**d** his nephew, Lot, who **h**ad been taken as a prisoner by four kings.

(14) _____ After the birth of Isaac, Sarah asked Abraham to **s**end Hagar and Ishmael away.

Abraham lived a full life, and when he died, his sons Isaac and Ishmael . . .

__ __ __ __ __ __ __ __ __

__ __ __ __ __ __ __ __ __ __.

(Genesis 25:7–10)

Moses is an Israelite born at a time when his people are slaves in <u>Egypt.</u> The Egyptian king, called the <u>Pharaoh</u>, is afraid of the growing number of Israelites. He orders all newborn boys to be drowned. The daughter of the Pharaoh saves <u>Moses</u>. She finds him in a basket in the river. She raises him as her own. This begins Moses' life. It is a life filled with challenges.

As an adult Moses runs away from Egypt. God appears to him and tells him to return to the Pharaoh. Moses is to deliver God's <u>demand</u> that the Pharaoh free the Israelites. God wants them to go to the land he has promised to Abraham and his descendants. Moses doubts he is the right person for the job. God, however, reminds him that he will have divine help. He also will have the help of Moses' brother, <u>Aaron.</u> Moses goes to see the Pharaoh. The Egyptian king quickly <u>refuses</u> Moses' request to free God's people.

God doesn't take no for an answer. He sends a series of disasters, called <u>plagues.</u> They force the Pharaoh to free the Israelites. With God's help, Moses leads the Israelites as they flee Egypt. They miraculously pass through the <u>Red Sea</u> and escape the Pharaoh's army. Once the Israelites are free, God makes a <u>covenant</u>, or sacred agreement, with them as God's Chosen People. To help the Israelites stay true to the Covenant, God gives Moses the sacred Law. It is summarized in the <u>Ten Commandments.</u>

Moses is one of the holiest saints of the Bible. But even with the Covenant and the Law, Moses finds that leading the Israelites through the desert to the Promised Land isn't easy. The <u>people complain and even betray</u> God. Moses does not live to enter the Promised Land. But until his death, Moses reminds the Israelites of the importance of keeping the Law and the Covenant.

The Law God gives the Israelites—<u>sometimes called the Old Law</u>—helps prepare us for the fulfillment of God's plan. In the Gospels Jesus teaches us God's New Law. We learn that Jesus does not put an end to the Old Law. Instead he shows us that love is the Law's true meaning (see Matthew 5:1—7:29).

Reflection

Look at the Ten Commandments in Exodus, chapter 20. Choose one commandment and write it down. Then brainstorm at least five ways we could observe this commandment in our modern lives. Repeat this process with the other commandments.

Bible Passages About Moses

Exodus 2:1–24
Moses grows up.

Exodus 3:1–22
God calls Moses.

Exodus 5:1–21
Moses and Aaron stand before the Pharaoh of Egypt.

Exodus 12:1–4
The Passover occurs.

Exodus 14:1–31
The Israelites cross the Red Sea.

Exodus 20:1–17
God gives the Ten Commandments.

MOSES

Put the events of Moses' life in the correct order of how they happened. You can figure this out by scanning the headlines in Exodus, chapters 1–20. Number the events 1 through 14 in the spaces provided. Starting with event number 1, put the bold, underlined letters in the spaces provided at the bottom. Some events have two letters in bold, underlined type. Be sure to put those letters in the spaces in the order in which they appear in the sentence.

(1) _____   In a pillar of cloud and a pill**a**r of **f**ire, the Lord guides Moses and the Israelites.

(2) _____   J**e**thro and Moses visit.

(3) _____   Moses a**n**d the Israelites arrive at Mount Sinai.

(4) _____   Moses and the Is**r**aelites cross the Red Sea.

(5) _____   Moses instru**c**ts the peopl**e** on what to do at the first Passover.

(6) _____   Moses is **f**loated down a river in a basket.

(7) _____   Moses kills **a** man and flees to Midian.

(8) _____   Moses meets **t**he king (pharaoh) of Egypt.

(9) _____   Moses receives the Ten Comman**d**ments.

(10) _____   Moses warns o**f** the de**a**th of the firstborn.

(11) _____   Water comes from a rock when Moses strikes **it**.

(12) _____   The Isra**e**lites are led out of Egypt by Mo**s**es.

(13) _____   The Lord **c**alls Mos**e**s at the burning bush.

(14) _____   The Lord strikes Egypt with plagues, **or** disasters.

Moses spoke with God . . .

__ __ __ __ __ __ __ __ __ __ __ __

__ __ __ __ __ __ __ __ __ __ __ __.

Leading the Israelites out of Egypt is only part of the work God gives Moses. Once the Israelites have escaped from Egypt, he still has to get them to the Promised Land. To do this Moses sends twelve men ahead to scout the land. They report that the land is wonderful. It is "rich and fertile" (Numbers 13:27). Still, most of the scouts advise against going into the land. They think the people there are too fierce and powerful to be defeated. Only two of the scouts, Joshua and Caleb, remember God's promises. They remember how he defeated the mighty Egyptian army. They argue that the Israelites can occupy the land if they trust God.

The Israelites refuse to listen to Joshua and Caleb. As a result, the people end up wandering in the desert. Forty more years pass before they enter the Promised Land.

At God's command, Moses makes Joshua the new leader of the Israelites before Moses dies. Moses led the Israelites safely through the Red Sea to escape the Egyptians. In the same way, Joshua, with God's help, leads the Chosen People across the Jordan River and into the Promised Land.

Once in the Promised Land, the heroic Joshua does not forget God or his Covenant and Law. Because of Joshua's constant faith, he leads the Israelites to victories over the people who live there. Most famously, he leads the Israelites in a march around the city of Jericho. The march leads to the city's walls falling down.

God promises Abraham land for all his descendants. Through Moses God delivers his Chosen People from slavery in Egypt. He gives them the Covenant and the Law. Faithful Joshua finally brings the Chosen People to the Promised Land. Interestingly, the name Joshua is another way to say the name Jesus. Both names mean "God saves."

Reflection

After reading the stories about Joshua, choose three qualities that make him a hero. Can you think of three other heroes or heroines (in history, film, or books) who also possess these qualities? What can all four heroes teach you?

Bible Passages About Joshua

Joshua, chapter 3
The Israelites cross the Jordan River.

Joshua, chapter 6
The Israelites capture Jericho.

Joshua 11:16–23
Joshua conquers the land.

Joshua 24:1–28
Joshua leads the renewal of the Covenant.

Joshua 24:29–31
Joshua dies.

JOSHUA

The story of Joshua starts in the Book of Exodus and continues in the Books of Numbers and Deuteronomy. The biggest part of Joshua's story, however, is found in the Book of Joshua. Answer the following about Joshua by looking up the verses indicated at the end of each line. To find out if you are correct, check for each of your answers in the word search. Put the unused letters from the word search in the spaces at the bottom of the page to spell out a fact about Joshua.

1. Joshua went up here with Moses. (8 letters) (Exodus 24:13)

2. Joshua was filled with this. (6 letters) (Deuteronomy 34:9)

3. Joshua sent two spies to go explore this city. (7 letters) (Joshua 2:1)

4. Joshua led the whole nation of Israel across this river. (6 letters) (Joshua 4:1)

5. Joshua ordered the people to shout and march around Jericho this many times. (5 letters) (Joshua 6:15–20)

6. Joshua read this aloud, including the blessings and the curses. (3 letters) (Joshua 8:34)

7. Joshua told the sun to do this. (two words, 10 letters) (Joshua 10:12)

8. Joshua divided the land among all the people of _____. (6 letters) (Joshua 11:23)

9. Joshua defeated many of these. (5 letters) (Joshua 12:7–24)

10. Joshua told the people to revere and honor the _____. (4 letters) (Joshua 24:14)

N	M	O	L	O	R	D	S	E	L
S	I	A	P	P	O	I	W	L	O
M	I	A	R	H	P	E	I	N	H
L	T	E	T	D	J	T	S	O	C
S	A	H	U	N	S	A	D	J	I
H	I	W	S	D	U	S	O	O	R
U	S	G	N	I	K	O	M	R	E
L	E	A	R	S	I	C	M	D	J
C	T	E	S	S	O	R	+	A	+
S	N	E	V	E	S	+	+	N	+

11. Joshua was buried in this hill country. (7 letters) (Joshua 24:30)

___ ___ ___ ___ ___   ___ ___ ___ ___   ___ ___ ___ ___ ___

___ ___ ___ ___ ___ ___   ___ ___ ___

___ ___ ___ ___ ___ ___ ___ ___ ___ ___.

Samson is a powerful man who helps save the Israelites from the Philistines. They are enemies of the Israelites. But this Bible hero is not always faithful, devoted, or even holy. He has human weaknesses and gives in to temptation. Still, God is willing to use this flawed individual. Samson can help fulfill God's plan for salvation.

At Samson's birth, his parents are thankful to God. In return they dedicate Samson to God by raising him as a Nazirite. Nazirites make a special commitment to God. They do not cut their hair, drink alcohol, or touch dead bodies. But Samson does not always keep the Nazirites' vows. He has a weakness for women. He can also be selfish. These problems often get Samson in trouble.

As a grown man, Samson is incredibly strong. Once he even kills a lion with his bare hands. Because of his great strength, and in spite of his weaknesses, Samson becomes a judge, or spirit-filled leader. He helps the Israelites defeat the Philistines. In one story he kills one thousand Philistines with the jawbone of a donkey.

In the middle of his battles against the Philistines, Samson falls in love with Delilah, a Philistine woman. She persuades him to reveal the secret of his strength. Samson tells Delilah that if his long hair is cut, he will lose his strength. That is because his uncut hair symbolizes his commitment to God.

Delilah betrays Samson by cutting his hair while he sleeps. The Philistines capture the now-weakened Samson. They take him to their temple. There they torture and make fun of this once-mighty leader of the Israelites. In his weakness, Samson prays to God for help. In one last burst of strength, he brings down the temple on the Philistines and himself. He loses his life but saves the Israelites.

Reflection

When Samson gets angry, he gets even. That often makes him forget his calling from God. What is your experience of anger that seeks to get even? Does anger solve problems? Does getting back at someone ever cause more problems? Explain.

Bible Passages About Samson

Judges 13:1–24
An angel announces Samson's birth to his parents.

Judges 14:1–20
Samson marries a Philistine woman, who betrays him.

Judges 15:1–8
Samson burns down the Philistines' orchards and fields.

Judges 15:9–20
Samson defeats the Philistines with a donkey's jawbone.

Judges 16:4–22
Delilah betrays Samson.

Judges 16:23–31
Samson defeats the Philistines and dies.

SAMSON

Samson was a judge of Israel. His story is in Judges, chapters 13–16. Read the story, and then complete the following activity. Rearrange the boxes to reveal facts about Samson.

In Judges 13:14 we find that:

NE	NOT	DRIN	WAS	K WI	F SA

ER O	MSON	MOTH	TO	THE

In Judges 14:6 we find that:

ANDS	WIT	S BA	RE H	APAR	SAMS

ORE	T A	LION	ON T	H HI

In Judges 15:14 we find that:

REAK	TO B	D MA	UGH	AMSO	THE

RONG	HAT	ES T	HIM	ENO	THE

HELD	N ST	LOR	ROP	DE S

In Judges 16:29–30 we find that:

ILDI	A BU	ED D	SAMS	NOCK	OWN

S	ON K	ILIS	ND K	E PH	TINE

NG A	ILLE	D TH

R uth is a simple woman from a foreign land. She plays a key role in the story of salvation. She is the great-grandmother of King David and a direct ancestor of Jesus.

Ruth's story begins in her homeland of Moab. This land is a neighbor to Israel and sometimes its enemy. Israel experiences a famine, or widespread starvation. One Israelite family moves to Moab. The family's sons marry Moabite women, Orpah and Ruth. Soon the father dies. His death leaves his wife, Naomi, to rely on her sons for support. But within ten years, the sons have died too.

After considering her situation, Naomi decides to return to Israel. She tells her daughters-in-law to return to their parents. A difficult life awaits Naomi in Israel. As a widow without male relatives, she will have no legal rights there. She also will be unable to support herself.

Ruth refuses to abandon Naomi, her mother-in-law, to such a future. Ruth pledges to stay with Naomi forever. This puts Ruth's needs aside and risks her future. The women return to Israel. Ruth accepts the faith of the Israelites.

In Israel, Ruth remains faithful to her promises to Naomi. To support herself and Naomi, Ruth works in the fields. She gathers leftover grain. Boaz witnesses Ruth's kindness and faithfulness. Boaz is a wealthy relative of Naomi's dead husband. He offers to marry Ruth.

Ruth comes to Israel as an outsider. She is accepted into God's people because she is a good and holy person who is faithful to her family and God. Ruth's story teaches that through faith, all people are part of God's family. Their cultural or ethnic backgrounds do not matter. In fact outsiders seem to have a special place in God's heart and God's plan.

In the story of Jesus' birth (see Matthew 1:5), we meet Ruth again. She is one of the few women listed in Jesus' family tree. Her presence there is a lasting sign that God works through both men and women. With them, he brings his Good News into the world.

Reflection

Ruth is an ordinary person. She helps her mother-in-law, Naomi, in an extraordinary way. When have you seen ordinary people do extraordinary things? How can you as an ordinary person help others in extraordinary ways?

Bible Passages About Ruth

Ruth 1:1–5
The people and the places are introduced.

Ruth 1:6–22
Naomi's sad situation and Ruth's generous response are described.

Ruth 2:1–23
Ruth gathers grain in Boaz's field.

Ruth 3:1–16
Ruth seeks to marry Boaz.

Ruth 4:1–12
Ruth marries Boaz.

RUTH

The Book of Ruth is a short but moving story of a young woman and her loyalty to her family. After reading Ruth, read the following "if-then" statements. Determine which statement is true and then place the correct letter in the spaces below in the order in which they occur to find out a fact about Ruth.

- ▶ If Elimelech and Naomi moved because of a famine, then 7 is R. If they moved because of an earthquake, then 7 is H.
- ▶ If Ruth was a Moabite, then 3 is E. If Ruth was an Israelite, then 3 is I.
- ▶ If Ruth's mother-in-law was Orpah, then 1 is T. If her mother-in-law was Naomi, then 1 is G.
- ▶ If Ruth returned to her own people, then 5 is K. If Ruth went with Naomi to Judah, then 5 is T.
- ▶ If Ruth continued to worship her own gods, then 13 is A. If Ruth chose the God of her mother-in-law, then 13 is T.
- ▶ If Ruth went to Jerusalem, then 10 is S. If Ruth went to Bethlehem, then 10 is D.
- ▶ If Boaz was the king, then 6 is V. If Boaz was a relative of Naomi, then 6 is G.
- ▶ If Ruth was forced to work in the fields, then 8 is I. If Ruth volunteered to work in the fields, then 8 is A.
- ▶ If Ruth helped plant the crop, then 2 is H. If Ruth walked behind the workers, picking up grain, then 2 is R.
- ▶ If Boaz told Ruth to work in his fields because she was a foreigner, then 4 is N. If Boaz told her to work in his fields because of all she had done for Naomi, then 4 is A.
- ▶ If Naomi advised Ruth not to work in Boaz's fields, then 9 is D. If Naomi told Ruth to continue working in Boaz's fields, then 9 is N.
- ▶ If Naomi planned to trick Boaz into giving them more food, then 11 is L. If Naomi planned to get Ruth married, then 11 is M.
- ▶ If Naomi told Ruth to lie at Boaz's feet, then 16 is R. If Ruth told Naomi to lie at Boaz's feet, then 16 is S.
- ▶ If Noami's closest relative gave Boaz his sandal, then 15 is E. If Ruth gave Boaz her sandal, then 15 is U.
- ▶ If Ruth married Boaz, then 12 is O. If Ruth married a closer relative, then 12 is Y.
- ▶ If Ruth had a son named Obed, then 14 is H. If Ruth had a daughter named Jesse, then 14 is F.

Ruth was the

__ __ __ __ __ - __ __ __ __ __ __ __ __ __ __
1   2   3   4   5   6   7   8   9 10 11 12 13 14 15 16

of King David.

The Israelite people considered King David to be their greatest leader and nation builder. David expands Israelite territory by defeating the enemies of Israel on all sides. David also brings together the twelve Tribes of Israel. He unites them into one nation, Israel. He brings peace and prosperity to the land. He even conquers the city of Jerusalem and turns it into the Israelites' capital city. Then he brings the sacred Covenant box, or ark, to Jerusalem. This becomes a holy city for all of Israel.

David is also remembered as a man devoted to God and a spiritual leader among the Israelites. While only a young man, David puts his total trust in God. Thus he can defeat the Philistine giant, Goliath. David is also a skilled musician. He loves to praise God in song and dance. He writes some of the earliest psalms. Out of respect for God, David refuses to harm King Saul when Saul tries to kill David. Even when David commits evil acts like adultery and murder, he admits his sins. In this way he accepts the consequences and recommits himself to God.

Since the time when David is a simple shepherd boy, God favors him. God promises to show David's descendants the same special care he gives David. In fact, God promises that David's descendants will rule a kingdom that will survive forever.

When David dies, the Israelites long for another leader just like him. They call this hoped-for leader the Messiah. Jesus, a descendant of David, is that longed-for Messiah. Jesus' obedience in dying on the cross establishes the true Kingdom of Heaven. Doing so fulfills God's promise to David to establish a Kingdom that will never end.

Reflection

Whom does everyone expect to win the battle between David and Goliath? Why does David win? What "Goliaths" do you face in your own life? What can you learn from this story that might help you better manage the battles in your life?

Bible Passages About David

1 Samuel 16:1–13
Samuel anoints David as king.

1 Samuel 17:41–54
David defeats Goliath.

1 Samuel 24:1–22
David spares Saul's life.

2 Samuel 5:1–16
David becomes king of Israel and Judah.

2 Samuel 7:1–17
Nathan sends a message to David about a Temple.

2 Samuel 11:1–27
David seduces Bathsheba.

2 Samuel 12:1–15
Nathan confronts David. David repents.

DAVID

The story of King David is told in detail in the Bible. In order to learn about David's life, try the following analogies. An analogy is a comparison showing how the relationship between two people or things is like the relationship between two other people or things. Here is an example of an analogy.

Abraham is to Isaac • as Jacob is to Joseph.

How do Abraham and Isaac compare with Jacob and Joseph? Abraham is the father of Isaac, and Jacob is the father of Joseph.

Try the following analogies regarding people, places, and events in David's life. The references in parentheses will help you discover the relationship.

1. Jonathan is to Saul   (1 Samuel 13:16)

    as Amnon is to _____.   (2 Samuel 3:2)

2. Kish is to Saul   (1 Samuel 9:1–2)

    as _____ is to David.   (1 Samuel 17:12)

3. Samuel is to Saul   (1 Samuel 10:1–2)

    as _____ is to David.   (1 Samuel 16:13)

4. Jonathan is to Michal   (1 Samuel 14:49)

    as Absalom is to _____.   (2 Samuel 13:1)

5. Nabal is to Abigail   (1 Samuel 25:14,39–42)

    as Uriah is to _____.   (2 Samuel 11:2–3,26–27)

6. Saul is to the Ammonites   (1 Samuel 11:11)

    as David is to the _____.   (2 Samuel 8:1)

7. Jerusalem is to Solomon   (2 Samuel 5:14)

    as _____ is to David.   (1 Samuel 17:12–15)

8. Nathan is to a prophet   (2 Samuel 7:2)

    as Joab is to a _____.   (2 Samuel 8:16)

Solomon is a son of David and the third king of Israel. When Solomon becomes king, God appears to him in a dream. He tells Solomon to ask for anything he wants. Solomon does not ask for riches or a long life. Instead he asks for the wisdom to be a good ruler. Solomon's choice pleases God. He promises Solomon the wisdom he asks for. On top of that, God rewards Solomon with riches and a long life.

Solomon uses his wisdom to strengthen Israel. He makes alliances with foreign kings by marrying their daughters. He then profits from the trade that crosses Israel's borders. In Israel's capital, Jerusalem, Solomon builds a great palace. He puts up defensive walls. Most important, he constructs a Temple for God.

Solomon's reputation spreads. People come from near and far to hear his words. The Bible honors his legendary wisdom. It names Solomon as the author of the Book of Proverbs, the Song of Songs, and the Book of Ecclesiastes.

Solomon's accomplishments come at a great price to the Israelites. He heavily taxes them. He forces them to work for months on his building projects. He chooses to build his own power and glory rather than remain faithful to God. Solomon turns his heart from God. He builds altars to the foreign gods his many wives worship.

Solomon's actions divide the Chosen People of God. God promised David his descendants would see a kingdom that would last forever. But Solomon turns away from God and follows his own ambitions. He does not fulfill God's promise.

When he dies, the ten northern tribes refuse to accept Solomon's son, Rehoboam, as their king. The Israelites' nation is split in two. The people will continue to wait for that promised descendant of David, the Messiah. They wish for him to fulfill God's promise for a kingdom that will last forever.

Reflection

Read 1 Kings 3:1–10. God asks Solomon what he wants. Solomon asks for wisdom. What do you think wisdom is? Is it only the same as being smart? If God invited you to ask for whatever you wanted, what would you ask for? Why?

Bible Passages About Solomon

1 Kings 3:1–15
Solomon prays for wisdom.

1 Kings 3:16–28
Solomon decides wisely for two mothers.

1 Kings 6:1–38
Solomon builds the Temple.

1 Kings 8:54–61
Solomon prays.

1 Kings 10:1–13
The Queen of Sheba visits.

1 Kings 11:1–13
Solomon turns away from God.

SOLOMON

The story of King Solomon is in 1 Kings, chapters 1–11. To complete the statements below, read the passages indicated at the end of each sentence. To find out if you are correct, check for each of your answers in the word search. Put the unused letters from the word search in the spaces at the bottom of the page to spell out a fact about Solomon. (All passages are in 1 Kings.)

1. Solomon was the son of
___ ___ ___ ___ ___. (2:12)

2. God told Solomon he would make him
___ ___ ___ ___. (3:12)

3. Solomon built the
___ ___ ___ ___ ___ ___. (6:1)

4. The Lord promised Solomon that if Solomon obeyed all God's commands, he would not forsake, or abandon,
___ ___ ___ ___ ___ ___. (6:11–13)

5. It took ___ ___ ___ ___ ___ years to build the Temple. (6:38)

6. Solomon also built a
___ ___ ___ ___ ___ ___ for himself. (7:1)

7. Solomon used ___ ___ ___ ___ ___ ___ labor to build the Temple and palace. (9:15)

8. Solomon was visited by the queen of ___ ___ ___ ___ ___. (10:1)

9. The ___ ___ ___ ___ ___ of Solomon led him into worship of other gods. (11:1–4)

10. ___ ___ ___ ___ ___ ___ ___ ___ led a revolt against Solomon. (11:26–27)

11. Solomon was king for ___ ___ ___ ___ ___ years. (11:42)

12. Solomon's son, ___ ___ ___ ___ ___ ___ ___ ___, became king after Solomon. (11:43)

T	S	S	O	L	D	O	J	M	M	O	E
E	N	W	H	W	A	E	A	S	R	I	C
M	C	H	I	E	R	O	C	E	R	A	A
P	N	S	D	O	B	W	I	R	F	S	L
L	E	E	B	O	R	A	T	O	O	D	A
E	H	O	H	L	E	A	R	S	I	F	P
A	A	E	N	A	N	T	Y	V	O	T	H
M	R	E	R	K	Y	I	A	N	G	+	+
N	E	V	E	S	+	D	S	E	V	I	W

— ___ ___ ___ ___ ___   ___ ___ ___ ___ ___ ___ ___ ___ ___

___ ___ ___ ___   ___ ___ ___ ___ ___ ___ ___ ___ ___

___ ___ ___ ___ ___ ___   ___ ___ ___ ___ ___ ___ ___ .

(1 Kings 10:23)

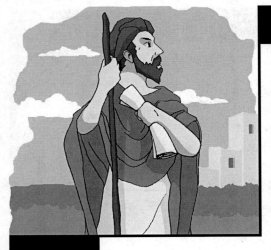

Prophets play an important part in salvation history. Their mission is to share the Word of God with the Chosen People. Isaiah becomes a prophet after experiencing a powerful vision of God in the Temple. The vision convinces him to put all his trust in God.

As a prophet, Isaiah advises the kings of God's Chosen People to rely on God in times of trial. He tells them to depend on God rather than on treaties with foreign nations. Isaiah warns the rich ruling class to stop mistreating the poor. Most important, Isaiah foretells the coming of a perfect ruler. This ruler will bring justice and peace for all.

Long after Isaiah dies, the Babylonians attack the Israelites. They capture the Israelites and bring them to Babylon as slaves. This captivity is often called the Exile. During the Exile, another prophet arises to comfort the people. He uses Isaiah's name and ideas. This "Second Isaiah" describes a servant of God whose suffering fulfills God's plan. God does not abandon the servant, says Second Isaiah. In the same way, he promises that God will rescue the people from their sufferings.

A third prophet also takes the name Isaiah. He celebrates this rescue when the Exile ends after about fifty years. Third Isaiah urges the people to practice justice toward one another. He predicts the coming of a great Kingdom.

The holy Isaiah and the prophets who later take his name promise that God will one day bring about a perfect Kingdom. They also share the story of a servant of God. This man will take on himself the sins of all. Through his suffering he will gain forgiveness for all. In this way he will fulfill God's plan for salvation. Jesus Christ is that Suffering Servant. He freely chooses to offer himself for the forgiveness of our sins. So he fulfills God's plan for salvation.

Reflection

The role of the prophet is like the role of a sports coach. Both people try to motivate people to "play up to their ability." Both combine warnings and encouragements. What personal coachlike qualities do you think a successful prophet should have?

Bible Passages About Isaiah

Isaiah 2:1–5
Isaiah predicts future peace to Jerusalem.

Isaiah 6:1–8
God calls Isaiah.

Isaiah 44:1–3
God consoles Israel.

Isaiah 49:1–6
Isaiah calls Israel a light to the nations.

Isaiah 52:13—53:12
Isaiah describes the Suffering Servant.

Isaiah 65:17–25
Isaiah predicts a new heaven, a new earth, and a new Jerusalem.

ISAIAH

The Book of Isaiah covers several hundred years in the history of Israel. It also records the preaching of several prophets. In it, the prophets speak of the sins of the people, the coming fall of the nation and the Exile, and the future of the people of God.

ACROSS

1. Isaiah said the ___ were misleading the people. (Isaiah 3:12)
3. Isaiah told of a child who would be born and would be called the Prince of ___. (Isaiah 9:5–6)
6. Isaiah spoke of new heavens and the new ___. (Isaiah 66:22)
8. God's love is compared to the love of a ___. (Isaiah 49:14–15)
9. Isaiah told the people that offering ___ to the hungry pleases God. (Isaiah 58:10)
12. Those who trust in the Lord and wait for him to save them will be taken up on ___ wings. (Isaiah 40:31)
13. The Lord appeared on a ___ to Isaiah. (Isaiah 6:1)
14. Isaiah told of a woman who would have a child and name him ___. (Isaiah 7:14)
15. The name of Isaiah's ___ was a prediction of what was to happen to Samaria. (Isaiah 8:3–4)

DOWN

1. An angel touched Isaiah's ___ with a burning coal or ember. (Isaiah 6:6–7)
2. In a vision, Isaiah saw flaming creatures with this number of wings. (Isaiah 6:2)
4. God told Isaiah to ___ his people. (Isaiah 40:1)
5. Isaiah said there would come a time when nations would no longer go to ___. (Isaiah 2:4)
7. Isaiah preached that God wanted the people to help the ___. (Isaiah 58:7)
9. Isaiah told the people what true ___ is. (Isaiah 58:1–7)
10. Isaiah replied to the Lord, "___ me!" (Isaiah 6:8)
11. Isaiah accused the people of spending time getting ___. (Isaiah 5:11)

E zekiel is a priest who becomes a prophet. He shares God's Word with the Israelites during times of sinfulness and despair. As a prophet, Ezekiel has his own unique ways of getting God's message across. For example, God makes Ezekiel speechless for a while. His lack of speech reminds the Israelites how they have ignored God's words.

In many courageous ways, Ezekiel tries to get the people's attention. Once he shaved his head and beard, as slaves and prisoners are forced to do. Then he burned his shaved hair as a sign of the hardships the Israelites will experience because of their sinful ways.

In his early years as a prophet, Ezekiel has a vision from God. It points out how evil and corrupt God's Chosen People have become. In his vision he sees God's presence leave the Temple in Jerusalem. The Israelites believed they would be safe as long as God's presence remained in the Temple. Ezekiel's hard message is that their sinfulness will have serious costs. The Babylonians destroy the Temple. The kingdom of the Israelites fails. Then the words of the prophet Ezekiel come true.

The Israelites live for many years in exile in Babylon. Ezekiel brings the people a new message from God. He describes a vision in which dead bones are brought to life. It is a sign of how God will one day restore Israel. He also promises that God will write a New Covenant on their hearts. These words bring the Israelites hope in difficult times.

In Jesus Christ we see the complete fulfillment of the prophet Ezekiel's words. In the Sermon on the Mount, Jesus teaches with the full authority of God, his Father. Jesus reminds us that good and evil actions have consequences. Christ has sent the Holy Spirit to empower us to live according to the New Covenant. He helps us keep the law of love in our hearts.

Reflection

God tells Ezekiel that his life as a prophet will be like this: "They will defy and despise you; it will be like living among scorpions. Still, don't be afraid of those rebels . . ." (Ezekiel 2:6). Knowing this, why do you think Ezekiel still accepts the call to be a prophet?

Bible Passages About Ezekiel

Ezekiel 1:1–28
Ezekiel sees God's throne.

Ezekiel 2:1–10
God calls Ezekiel.

Ezekiel 3:1–15
Ezekiel eats a scroll and receives God's Spirit.

Ezekiel 34:11–31
God is the Good Shepherd.

Ezekiel 36:22–36
God will give the people a new heart and mind.

Ezekiel 37:1–14
Ezekiel describes a vision of the dry bones.

EZEKIEL

The prophet Ezekiel had many visions as he preached to the people of Judah. Read the passages from Ezekial for each statement below, and then complete the statement. To find out if your answers are correct, check for each of your answers in the word search. Put the unused letters from the word search in the spaces at the bottom of the page to spell out a fact about Ezekiel.

1. Ezekiel was among the ___ at the River Chebar. (6 letters) Ezekiel 1:1

2. Ezekiel saw ___ in a vision. (6 letters) Ezekiel 1:15–21

3. Ezekiel was told in one of his visions to eat a ___. (6 letters) Ezekiel 2:1–10

4. To symbolize the sins of Israel, God told Ezekiel to build a miniature of Jerusalem and lie on his ___. (4 letters) Ezekiel 4:1–8

5. Ezekiel was to cut his ___ and scatter it in the miniature city he made. (4 letters) Ezekiel 5:1–4

6. God showed Ezekiel a ___ in a wall that led to the Temple. (4 letters) Ezekiel 8:7

```
E  Z  E  K  I  T  S  C  R  O  L  L
E  L  W  A  S  N  A  P  R  G  E  O
J  E  R  U  S  A  L  E  M  L  V  P
H  E  T  T  S  N  O  J  U  O  I  D
A  H  A  S  N  E  D  W  A  R  L  S
T  H  O  L  E  V  N  A  K  Y  E  N
I  N  T  E  O  O  E  O  H  A  I  R
E  X  I  E  L  C  E  X  B  I  N  B
D  R  E  H  P  E  H  S  I  Y  A  B
Y  L  O  W  N  +  +  I  +  L  R  +
E  L  P  M  E  T  +  D  +  +  E  D
+  +  +  +  +  +  +  E  +  +  +  S
```

7. In one of his visions, Ezekiel saw the ___ of God leaving the Temple in Jerusalem. (5 letters) Ezekiel 10:15–18

8. God promised to establish an everlasting ___ with Israel. (8 letters) Ezekiel 16:59–60

9. God told Ezekiel that he wanted Israel to change its ___ ways. (4 letters) Ezekiel 33:10–11

10. Ezekiel learned of the fall of the city of ___. (9 letters) Ezekiel 33:21

11. In one of Ezekiel's visions, God compared himself to a ___. (8 letters) Ezekiel 34:11–16

12. Ezekiel saw a vision of ___ that came to life. (8 letters) (2 words) Ezekiel 37:1–14

13. Ezekiel had a vision of a new ___. (6 letters) Ezekiel 40:1–7

— — — — — — — — — — —

— — — — — — — — — — — —

— — — — — — — — — — — — —

— — — — — — —

— — — — — — — — .

The Israelite people suffer fifty years of captivity in Babylon. The suffering ends when the Persians conquer Babylon. They set the Israelites free. Returning home means the Israelites must face the huge challenge of rebuilding their nation. It will take tough, physical labor to restore Jerusalem. They must rebuild its protective walls and its Temple. The Israelites will also struggle with a spiritual task. This is the renewing of their commitment to the Covenant, their laws, and religious practices.

Ezra and Nehemiah are leaders known for their holiness and commitment to God's people. Ezra is a priest and a man dedicated to studying and practicing God's Law. Nehemiah is also a man of faith. He commits himself to restoring Jerusalem and God's Chosen People. Both men serve Persian emperors. They receive permission to return to Israel a few generations after the first Israelites returned from captivity. There they will help the rebuilding efforts.

Together, Ezra and Nehemiah achieve great things. Under their leadership, the rebuilding of Jerusalem and the Temple is completed. They appoint scribes and judges to establish law and order. They restore the identity of the Israelite nation, nearly lost during the Exile. They do so by removing all foreign influences from their midst. They especially focus on foreign wives.

Most important, Ezra and Nehemiah work to renew the spiritual foundation of the Israelite people. Ezra reads the Covenant to the people. Both leaders stress the importance of obeying God's Law.

Before the Exile, the Israelites were united under kings like David and Solomon. After the Exile, the Israelites no longer are an independent nation. Yet, Ezra and Nehemiah lead the people to a new unity. It is based on their common faith and the worship of their God.

Jesus announces God's Kingdom on this same spiritual base. It does not rest on the power of kings. For those who follow Jesus, then and now, that rule is based not on power but on love.

Reflection

Ezra and Nehemiah help rebuild Jerusalem after its people return from the Exile. Think of people whose homes were flooded or destroyed by Hurricane Katrina in 2005. Or consider some other recent disaster. What challenges do these people face in rebuilding their cities and towns? How can we help them with their rebuilding?

Bible Passages About Ezra and Nehemiah

Ezra 1:1–10
Cyrus sends the Jews back to Jerusalem.

Ezra 7:1–10
Ezra's background is described.

Ezra 9:1—10:17
Ezra leads the people in denouncing mixed marriages.

Nehemiah, chapters 1–2
Nehemiah returns to Judah to help rebuild Jerusalem.

Nehemiah 10:28–39
The people of Jerusalem promise to reform their ways.

Nehemiah, chapter 13
Nehemiah reforms the people of Jerusalem.

EZRA AND NEHEMIAH

Ezra and Nehemiah were leaders of the Jews after the Exile in Babylon. Each has a book in the Old Testament named for him.

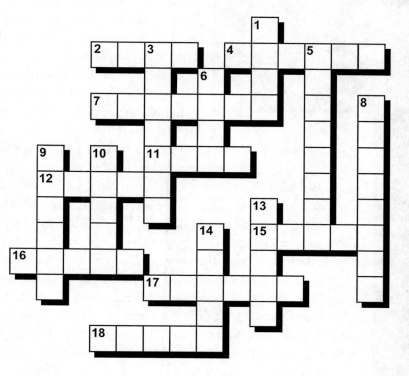

ACROSS

2. Ezra called for the people to ___ and pray for God to protect them. (Ezra 8:21–23)
4. When the Jews returned to Jerusalem from Babylon, they rebuilt the ___. (Ezra 3:8–10)
7. People of the area plotted to fight against the Jews because they did not want them to ___ the city. (Nehemiah 4:1–3)
11. The people answered "___" to Ezra. (Nehemiah 8:6)
12. The people promised to dedicate the ___ born of each family to God. (Nehemiah 10:36–37)
15. Ezra was a descendant of this high priest. (Ezra 7:1–5)
16. Ezra was unhappy because some of the Jews had foreign ___. (Ezra 9:1–2)
17. When the Jews returned to Jerusalem, they found that the gates of the city had been ___. (Nehemiah 1:1–3)
18. Nehemiah and others worked to rebuild the ___ of the city of Jerusalem. (Nehemiah 2:17)

DOWN

1. Ezra ___ the Law to the people. (Nehemiah 8:1–3)
3. Nehemiah told the people not to work or sell anything on the ___. (Nehemiah 13:15–18)
5. The people began to celebrate this festival again when they returned to Jerusalem. (Ezra 6:19)
6. Nehemiah said he would stand up to his enemies and not ___ in the Temple. (Nehemiah 6:10–11)
8. Nehemiah was ___ of Judah. (Nehemiah 5:14)
9. People living around the Jews tried to make the Jews too ___ to keep building. (Ezra 4:4)
10. Some of the people in the area ___ to complain about the Jews rebuilding the Temple. (Ezra 4:6)
13. Nehemiah ordered the doors to the city ___ shut at the beginning of the Sabbath. (Nehemiah 13:19)
14. This king allowed the Jews in exile to return to Jerusalem. (Ezra 1:1–4)

For almost four hundred years, the Israelites live peacefully. They accept the rule of many foreign powers. But one especially demanding Greek leader forces the Israelites to adopt Greek culture. He makes them worship Greek gods. He outlaws the Israelites' religious practices. Furthermore, he puts a statue of the Greek god Zeus in the Temple in Jerusalem.

Finally, a Greek official tries to force an Israelite priest named Mattathias to offer a sacrifice to a pagan god. Mattathias kills the official. His act starts an Israelite revolt that his five sons lead. These revolutionaries become known as the Maccabees. The word means "hammer." It also describes the power of their attacks.

The Old Testament Books of Maccabees tell how determinedly many holy and heroic Israelites fight for their religious freedom. One story tells of a mother and her seven sons. They are arrested and tortured. This treatment is meant to force them to break God's Law. But each in turn accepts death rather than turn away from God. They go to their deaths speaking to the king. They agree that he is taking their lives. But they say God will raise them up again to live forever. Their response shows their belief in God's final victory over death.

The Maccabees live in difficult times. Powerful foreigners surround them. These people have different lifestyles. They want everyone they control to do the same as they do. The Maccabees do not take the easy way out by giving up their faith in God and his Law. Instead they fight for religious freedom. Their courage inspires the Israelite people to hold firm to God and his Law. By their example, the Maccabees play an important part in salvation history. They help keep the Chosen People faithful to their calling.

Reflection

The Greeks try to force their religious beliefs on the Israelites. The Maccabees defend their faith. They revolt against the Greeks. Where do you think the Maccabees get their strength and the courage to stand up for their beliefs? How do you react when others use peer pressure to force you to give up on your faith?

Bible Passages About The Maccabees

1 Maccabees 1:20–53
Antiochus persecutes the Jews.

1 Maccabees 2:15–28
Mattathias refuses to submit to the Greeks.

1 Maccabees 3:1–9,
2 Maccabees 8:1–7
Judas leads victories against the Israelites' enemies.

1 Maccabees 4:36–59,
2 Maccabees 10:1–8
The Temple is purified and rededicated.

2 Maccabees 12:38–45
Judas encourages his soldiers to pray for their dead comrades.

THE MACCABEES

The Maccabean Revolt is named for the nickname of one of its heroes, Judas Maccabeus. Maccabeus means "hammer" and Judas was a ferocious fighter. His father, his five brothers, and Judas led the Jews in a war for religious and political freedom from their cruel Greek rulers. All passages are from 1 Maccabees.

1.   M __ __ __ __ __ __ __ __ __

2.   __ __ __   A __

3.   __ __ __ __ __   C __ __ __

4.   __ __ __ __ __ __ __   C __ __ __ __

5.   __ __ __   A __ __ __

6.   B __ __ __

7.   __ __ __   E

8.   __ __ __ __ __ __   E __

9.   S __ __ __ __

1. This priest sparked the beginning of the revolt. (2:15–28)

2. He took command after his father died. (3:1–2)

3. This king was furious with the Jewish revolt and put together a large army to fight the Jews. (3:27–28)

4. Judas and his men secured Jerusalem and purified the Temple and _____ the altar (sanctuary). (4:36–61)

5. This son of Mattathias sacrificed his life in the revolt. (6:32–46)

6. Nicanor led his army to Jerusalem and threatened to _____ the Temple. (7:26–38)

7. Judas and the Jews made an alliance, or treaty, with _____. (8:1–22)

8. Trypho killed Jonathan and sent troops here to kill his soldiers. (12:39–53)

9. This brother took over and finally succeeded in winning the revolt. (13:15–16)

Read 1 Maccabees 13:31–42. In what year did the Jews win their battle for freedom?

_____

Checking the footnotes of your Bible, what year is that in the current calendar?

_____

The New Testament contains twenty-seven books. Each one was written with the Holy Spirit's inspiration. These books contain several kinds of writings. You will find the Gospels, religious history, and letters to individuals and communities. Also included are homilies and visions. All these books are in some way about God's biggest breakthrough in history: Jesus Christ. The New Testament stories tell how Jesus' mission starts with God's Chosen People. Today we know these people as the Jews. The stories also tell how Jesus' first disciples quickly expand the mission to include non-Jews. These people are called Gentiles.

Testament is another word for *covenant*. A covenant is a holy promise made between God and human beings. The Old Testament is about the original Covenant God made with his Chosen People. The New Testament shows how Jesus Christ fulfills the promises of the Covenant in the Old Testament. Through Jesus, God extends the Covenant to the whole human race. We call this the New Covenant. It is a promise that every person—Jew or Gentile—can have eternal life with God. This New Testament tells how Jesus' life, death, and Resurrection made this possible.

To fully understand God's plan for the human race, we need both the Old and the New Testaments. The New Testament reveals the great love God has for us, shown by sending his Son into the world. Through the Gospels and letters, God shows us we can be saved from fear, anxiety, sin, and even death. We do this by putting our faith in Jesus Christ. Then as disciples empowered by the Holy Spirit, we follow the example of the holy men and women of the Bible in bringing God's love to other people.

Reflection

Page through the New Testament of your Bible. What stories do you recognize? If you have any favorite stories in the New Testament, what are they? What do they teach you about Jesus Christ?

Sections of the New Testament

The New Testament is usually divided into two or three main sections. Here's some information on each section:

The Gospels and the Acts of the Apostles. The word *gospel* literally means "good news." We call Matthew, Mark, Luke, and John Gospels because they uniquely tell the Good News: the life and mission of Jesus Christ. For this reason the four Gospels are considered the heart of the Bible. Many scholars believe Mark was written first. The writers of Matthew and Luke probably used Mark as a starting point to create their Gospels. That is why these three Gospels have some similar stories.

The Gospel of John is different from the other three. There are fewer miracles and fewer parables. John more clearly presents Jesus as God's Son. Having four Gospels gives us a more complete understanding of Jesus than if we had just one.

The Acts of the Apostles picks up where the Gospels leave off. The same person who wrote the Gospel of Luke also wrote this book. Acts tells the exciting story of the first Christians. By traveling and preaching, they spread the Good News of Jesus Christ throughout the known world.

The Letters. At the time of Jesus, there was no telephone, television, radio, or Internet. The early leaders of the Church had to communicate by writing letters. They wrote to groups and individuals. These letters helped the first Christians understand what being a follower of Jesus meant. The letters continue to help us today.

Saint Paul, or people writing in his name, wrote most of the letters. It was common at that time to honor a great person by writing letters or books in the person's name.

Revelation. The Revelation to John is not a letter. Instead, it is a collection of prophecies and visions. It is about the struggle between good and evil in the world. Revelation shows that believers will suffer and be mistreated, or persecuted. Yet it also promises that God will make everything right in the end.

Turn to the table of contents in the beginning of your Bible and use it and the books of the New Testament to answer the following questions on the New Testament.

1. How many books are in the New Testament?_____

2. What is the first book of the New Testament?_____

3. What is the last book of the New Testament?_____

4. Which book in the New Testament is the longest?_____

5. Which book in the New Testament is the shortest?_____

6. List the four Gospels.

   _____, _____

   _____, _____

7. List at least three letters (Epistles).

   _____, _____, _____

8. What book comes right after the Gospel of John?_____

Now try looking up some Bible passages. Look up each passage below and write the word indicated to complete a sentence about the New Testament.

9. Matthew 4:7   Write the first word of the passage in the space before the (9).

10. Romans 8:10   Write the third word of the passage in the space before the (10).

11. Mark 14:12   Write the third word of the passage in the space before the (11).

12. Acts 11:26   Write the last word of the passage in the space before the (12).

The New Testament tells us about

_____(9)

_____(10)

and the_____(11)

_____(12).

In the story of salvation, God works through no woman as powerfully as he does through Mary of Nazareth. The Gospel of Luke tells us Mary is a poor Jewish teenager. She lives a simple life in the small town of Nazareth. Yet to this young woman, an angel of God comes with an incredible request.

God asks Mary to give birth to the long-awaited Messiah. This is the Savior that God promised to the Chosen People through the prophets of Israel. God's words must shock and trouble Mary. At the time she is unmarried, although she is engaged to a man named Joseph.

Mary is unlike Adam and Eve. At the beginning of creation, they rejected God's plan. Instead Mary puts all her trust in God. She shows her trust by agreeing to become the mother of Jesus Christ. By her yes, Mary is truly the Mother of God. She is the mother of the eternal Son of God, made man for our sake.

After giving birth to Jesus, Mary faces many of the same problems any parent faces. In one instance the family makes a religious trip to Jerusalem. While returning to Nazareth, Mary and Joseph discover that Jesus has been left behind in the Jerusalem Temple. Imagine how frightening that must have been.

From the Gospels we learn that Mary is also present at key moments in Jesus' adult life. She is there when Jesus works his first miracle at the wedding feast in Cana. Sadly, she is also there when he is crucified.

Mary is truly a holy woman. God blesses her in many ways. From the very moment of her conception in her mother's womb, she is kept free from Original Sin. She remains without sin her whole life. Mary is also with the Apostles when the Holy Spirit descends on them at Pentecost. At her death, she becomes the first person to experience the resurrection of the body. She is taken, body and soul, up into heaven. There she shares in the glory of Christ's Resurrection. She waits with Jesus and all the saints for us to join them.

Reflection

Mary discovers Jesus is not among their group traveling from Jerusalem (see Luke 2:41–52). She is worried. Jesus would have been just about your age then. How do parents react today when their children become lost or separated from them? How can you help adults who care for you not to have that kind of worry?

Bible Passages About Mary of Nazareth

Matthew 1:18–25,
Luke 2:4–20
Jesus is born.

Luke 1:26–38
The angel makes the Annunciation.

Luke 1:39–56
Mary visits Elizabeth. She sings the *Magnificat*.

Luke 2:41–52
Jesus remains in the Temple to teach.

John 2:1–12
The wedding in Cana takes place.

John 19:25–27
Mary is present at the cross.

MARY OF NAZARETH

Mary is the mother of Jesus and so, the Mother of God. Read the passages indicated at the end of the statements and complete this activity by filling in the answers to the clues.

1. __ __ M __ __ __
2. __ O __ __ __ __
3. __ __ T __ __ __
4. __ __ __ H __ __ __ __ __
5. __ __ __ __ __ __ E __ __
6. __ __ __ __ R __ __ __

    O

    F

7. G __ __ __ __ __ __
8. __ O __ __ __ __ __ __ __
9. __ __ __ __ __ D

1. This man was in the Temple when Mary brought Jesus there as a baby. He told Mary that Jesus was a sign from God. (Luke 2:25–35)

2. He was the husband of Mary. (Matthew 1:18–24)

3. At his mother's request, Jesus turned this into wine at a wedding in Cana. (John 2:1–10)

4. This is where Mary gave birth to Jesus. (Luke 2:1–7)

5. This is the cousin of Mary whom Mary visited while she was pregnant. (Luke 1:39–45)

6. This is the hometown of Mary. (Luke 2:39)

7. This angel came to Mary to announce the birth of Jesus. (Luke 1:26–38)

8. Through his power Mary conceived Jesus. (Matthew 1:20)

9. Elizabeth called Mary this. (Luke 1:42)

A true hero of our faith, John the Baptist is a cousin to Jesus. His preaching sets the stage for Jesus' ministry. Like some Old Testament heroes, he is born to a childless couple. His birth fulfills an angel's prediction.

As a grown man, John leads an unusual life. He dresses simply. He eats off the land and preaches in the desert. So powerful is John's witness that people come out to the desert to see if he might be the Messiah. John assures them his job is only to prepare the way for the true Messiah.

John tells the people to be ready for the Messiah. He says they must repent and turn away from sin. They must treat one another more justly. Those with food and clothes should give to those in need. Those in positions of power should stop mistreating the weak.

In the Jordan River, John baptizes the people who repent of their sins. Their baptisms are signs of how they have been washed clean of their sins. Even though he is without sin, Jesus comes to be baptized by John. In this way he shows his full commitment to serving God the Father. When Jesus emerges from the water, the Holy Spirit comes down on him. God the Father speaks his approval.

John the Baptist calls King Herod to repent of his sins. The king is angry. He arrests and executes John. Before he dies, John sends his disciples to ask Jesus if he is the Messiah. John's disciples report back how Jesus heals the sick and preaches good news to the poor. These are signs for John that the Messiah has indeed come.

Through the prophets, God promises his Chosen People he will send a messenger to announce the coming of the Messiah. John is that messenger. Jesus himself gives John the ultimate seal of approval: "I assure you that John the Baptist is greater than anyone who has ever lived" (Matthew 11:11).

Reflection

John the Baptist feels most comfortable spending time with God in the desert. What place draws you to spend time with God? Describe it in words or illustrate it.

Bible Passages About John the Baptist

Matthew 3:1–12, Mark 1:1–8, Luke 3:1–18, John 1:19–28
John the Baptist preaches in the wilderness.

Matthew 3:13–17, Mark 1:9–11, Luke 3:21–22
Jesus is baptized.

Matthew 11:1–19, Luke 7:18–35
John sends messengers to speak with Jesus.

Matthew 14:1–12, Mark 6:14–29, Luke 9:7–9
John dies.

Luke 1:5–25
John's birth is announced.

Luke 1:57–80
John the Baptist is born.

John 3:22–30
John's relationship to Jesus is described.

Stories of John the Baptist are in all four Gospels. Read the listed passages about John the Baptist and finish the statements below. To find out if your answers are correct, check for each of your answers in the word search. Put the unused letters from the word search in the spaces at the bottom of the page to spell out a fact about John the Baptist.

Reading List
Matthew 3:1–6 and 11:2–6
Mark 6:17–29
Luke 1:57–63 and 3:15–20
John 1:29

J	S	O	C	H	L	N	T	E	H	D
E	W	B	A	A	A	P	T	L	I	I
Z	E	S	M	T	M	W	S	I	N	S
E	N	A	E	S	B	A	D	Z	N	C
C	D	C	L	D	O	O	E	A	A	I
H	O	U	S	O	F	S	S	B	D	P
A	O	I	H	R	G	N	E	E	R	L
R	G	O	A	E	O	F	R	T	O	E
I	J	E	I	H	D	S	T	H	J	S
A	U	P	R	I	S	O	N	S	+	+
H	E	A	D	+	+	+	+	+	+	+

1. The father of John the Baptist
   (9 letters)
2. The mother of John the Baptist
   (9 letters)
3. John was baptizing at this river.
   (6 letters)
4. John the Baptist was murdered by chopping off this.
   (4 letters)
5. John criticized him for marrying his brother's wife. (5 letters)
6. John preached this.
   (8 letters, 2 words)
7. King Herod put John here. (6 letters)
8. John spent time living here.
   (6 letters)
9. John baptized people and told them to repent, or turn away, from this. (4 letters)
10. John called Jesus this. (9 letters, 3 words)
11. John sent some of these men to talk with Jesus. (9 letters)
12. John wore clothes made of this. (10 letters, 2 words)

__ __ __ __ __ __ __ __ __ __ __ __ __ __ __

__ __ __ __ __ __ __ __ __

__ __ __ __ __ __ __ __.

The Gospels agree that Jesus' family was like no other. Certainly circumstances surrounding the birth of Jesus are miraculous. Jesus is unlike any other human being. He is conceived by the power of the Holy Spirit. He is not conceived by the ordinary union of a man and a woman. Blessed in this unique way by God, Mary and Joseph accept their relationship with amazing faith in God's plan for their family. They devote themselves to raising Jesus.

At the time of Jesus' birth, King Herod becomes alarmed by the predicted birth of a Messiah. He orders the killing of infant boys. He hopes to rid the country of any future challenge to his rule. Mary and Joseph take Jesus and flee to safety in Egypt. Finally Herod's death makes it safe for them to return to Nazareth.

There is only one other story of Jesus' family life. It takes place on the family's return from the Passover feast in Jerusalem. Joseph and Mary discover that the twelve-year-old Jesus has been left behind. They return to Jerusalem to search for Jesus. They find him in the Temple among the teachers. They are amazed at his understanding of the Scriptures.

This single story tells us that Jesus is being raised in a family where religion is taken seriously. It also reveals that even at a young age, Jesus is already turning his life toward the work of his heavenly Father.

No other Gospel stories tell of the life of Jesus during his childhood or teen years. We can assume Jesus lives like a typical Jewish boy growing up in a faith-filled family. Above all, the Gospels tell us that when God's time is right, his only Son, the eternal Word, becomes incarnate. That is, without losing his divine nature, he takes on our human nature. Jesus Christ is true God and true man. Because of this, he is the only one who can bridge the separation between God and humanity that Original Sin caused.

Reflection

Luke 2:41–52 talks about the boy Jesus in the Temple. Jesus is still in Jerusalem because he is becoming a leader in his faith. He is learning from adult leaders in the Temple. How can you be a leader in your faith in school, among friends, in your family, or at church?

Bible Passages About Jesus and His Family

Matthew 1:1–17
The ancestors of Jesus Christ are named.

Matthew 2:1–12
Visitors arrive from the East.

Matthew 2:13–23
The Holy Family escapes to Egypt.

Matthew 1:18–25, Luke 2:1–7
Jesus Christ is born.

Luke 2:8–20
The shepherds and the angels worship the baby Jesus.

Luke 2:21–38
Jesus is named and presented in the Temple.

Luke 2:41–52
The boy Jesus teaches in the Temple.

John 1:1–14
The Word becomes a human being.

JESUS AND HIS FAMILY

Two of the four Gospels have stories about Jesus' birth. Only one Gospel has a story about Jesus as a child. In these stories we also learn more about Mary, Jesus' mother, and Joseph, his foster father. Read Matthew, chapters 1–2, and Luke, chapter 2, and then complete this crossword. Because Matthew and Luke tell different stories about Jesus' birth, some answers will be found in only one of these Gospels.

ACROSS

4. In Luke, we learn that Jesus grew in favor with ____ and people.
8. Age at which Jesus went with his parents to Jerusalem for the Passover
10. This being appeared to the shepherds and announced Jesus' birth.
12. The visitors who studied the stars followed this to find Jesus.
15. There was no room here for Mary and Joseph.
17. When Mary and Joseph found the young Jesus, who had been lost, he described the Temple as his ____'s house.
18. Jesus was born in this town.
19. An angel appeared to Joseph in a ____ and told him that it was safe to return to Israel.
20. "Crib" for the baby Jesus
21. The angel of the Lord announced that a ____ was born in the city of David.

DOWN

1. Orders were given to kill all the boys in Bethlehem who were ____ years old or younger.
2. Men who studied the stars traveled from this direction to see the baby Jesus.
3. One of Jesus' ancestors was ____ David.
5. Joseph and Mary offered a sacrifice of a pair of these when Jesus was presented in the Temple.

6. One of the gifts given to the baby Jesus
7. He was thankful that he lived long enough to see the Messiah.
9. Joseph took Jesus and Mary here to protect them.
10. First person in the line of the ancestors of Jesus
11. It took Joseph and Mary this many days to find Jesus in the Temple.
13. Joseph and Mary found Jesus talking with these people in the Temple.
14. This king wanted to kill the newborn Jesus.
16. Town in which Jesus grew up

Jesus shares the Good News about the Kingdom of God with all who will listen. For some people, the word kingdom brings to mind particular images. They may include the picture of a ruler dressed in royal clothing and living in a castle. They may include images of a ruler who demands hard work and taxes from his subjects.

Jesus talks about a very different kind of Kingdom. Jesus teaches that the Kingdom of God exists wherever and whenever people truly live out God's law of love.

Sometimes, to get his message across, Jesus uses special stories called parables. When Jesus shares a parable, it is usually based on everyday life. It often has a surprising twist or unexpected ending. This twist gets people to see common things in a whole new way. Jesus' parables teach us that in God's Kingdom, the poor and forgotten are cared for and sinners are forgiven. The parables teach that the citizens of God's Kingdom are those who hear Jesus, believe in him, and follow him.

At other times Jesus uses more than just words to share his message. He also uses his miraculous healing power to accomplish his goals. His healings are true miracles. The blind can see, the lame can walk, and lepers are cured of their diseases. The people are amazed at the extraordinary cures Jesus works. But Jesus doesn't perform healing miracles just to get attention.

Jesus heals so that we come to understand the true nature of God's Kingdom. Sometimes he even breaks religious laws to heal someone. His healing miracles demonstrate clearly that love rules the Kingdom of God. This love puts the good of people above everything else.

Through his parables and miracles in the Gospels, Jesus, the Master Teacher and divine Miracle Worker, teaches us the importance of faith. What is necessary for healing and for entering the Kingdom of God is belief in Jesus and faith in the power of God.

Reflection

Imagine you were a disciple during Jesus' earthly years. Then imagine you heard him tell a parable and watched him perform a healing miracle. Would you be more interested in listening to him speak or in watching him perform a healing? Explain.

Bible Passages About Jesus' Teachings and Miracles

Matthew 6:25–33, Luke 12:22–31, Luke 16:13
Jesus tells how God views possessions.

Matthew 13:44–46
Jesus tells the parables of the hidden treasure and the pearl.

Matthew 19:22–26, Mark 10:23–27, Luke 18:24–27
Jesus tells the parable of the rich man.

Matthew 22:34–40, Mark 12:28–34, Luke 10:25–28
Jesus gives the Great Commandment.

Matthew 25:31–46
Jesus describes the Final Judgment.

Matthew 8:5–13, Luke 7:1–10
Jesus heals a centurion's servant.

Matthew 9:1–8, Mark 2:1–12, Luke 5:17–26
Jesus heals a paralyzed man.

Matthew 20:29–34, Mark 10:46–52, Luke 18:35
Jesus heals a blind beggar.

Mark 1:21–28, Luke 4:31
Jesus heals a man with an unclean spirit.

JESUS' TEACHINGS AND MIRACLES

Jesus teaches about the Kingdom of God through his parables and miracles. Below are Bible passages followed by a statement about each passage. Find and read the Bible passages, and then complete the statements by unscrambling the jumbled word in each. Put the numbered letters in the proper spaces below to learn a fact about the Kingdom of God.

Matthew 6:31–33

We should put the Kingdom of God before *V T N Y E E H I R G*.

— — — — —(16)— — —(3)(8)—

Matthew 13:44–46

The Kingdom of God is a great *E A U R R S E T* that brings happiness.

— — —(14)(7)— — — —

Matthew 25:34–40

We will bring about the Kingdom of God if we help and care for *H O T E S R*.

— — — —(9)—(12)

Mark 10:23–27

Entering the Kingdom of God will be difficult for a *H R C I* person.

— —(10)(5)

Matthew 8:5–13

A Roman officer or centurion asked Jesus to heal his *T A N V E S R*.

(13)(11)— — — — —

Mark 2:1–12

Four men opened a *O F R O* to lower a sick man to Jesus.

— — —(1)

Luke 18:35–43

Jesus told a beggar that his *I H A F T* made him able to see.

—(2)(6)—

Luke 4:31–37

The people were amazed because Jesus spoke with *Y R U I O T T A H*.

— — — — —(15)—(4)—

The parables and miracles of Jesus teach us that . . .

(1)(2)(3)(4)(5) (6)(7) (8)(9)(10)(11)(12)(13)(14)(15)(16)

. . . for entering the Kingdom of God.

Jesus dies in one of the most painful ways human beings have ever created, by crucifixion. In the midst of a ministry of love, Jesus is arrested, convicted of blasphemy, and nailed to a cross. His torture and death come not because of any crime he commits. They occur as the result of sinful human behavior. Like the Suffering Servant the prophet Isaiah describes, Jesus takes on himself the sins of others to save them.

The Gospels report in detail the events surrounding the suffering and death of Jesus. This is because his suffering and death were important to his followers. They did not expect their Messiah, our Savior, to experience so much suffering and death. Eventually they came to see that the Son of God made man really died and was buried to save us all.

On the third day, Jesus rises from the dead and appears to his good friend, the faithful Mary Magdalene. Later he appears to the Apostles. Then, according to Saint Paul, the risen Christ appears to more than five hundred eyewitnesses at the same time (see 1 Corinthians 15:6).

We don't know what Jesus' body looked like after his Resurrection. Mary Magdalene doesn't recognize him at first. Jesus joins two of his disciples walking along the road to Emmaus. They don't recognize him either at first. They finally do as he explains the Scriptures to them and breaks bread with them. By his Resurrection appearances, Jesus convinces even the doubtful among his followers that he truly has risen from the dead. Forty days after his Resurrection, Jesus ascends into Heaven. There he sits at God's right hand until he comes again in glory.

When each of us dies, Christ will judge us by comparing our lives to the Gospel message. This is called the particular judgment. Saint Paul described it this way: "For all of us must appear before Christ, to be judged by him. We will each receive what we deserve, according to everything we have done, good or bad, in our bodily life" (2 Corinthians 5:10).

In the Gospel of Matthew, Jesus describes a second judgment, called the Last Judgment, when God's plan for creation will be fully realized. At the last judgment, the king on his throne—who is Jesus Christ—will separate people into two groups, the righteous people on his right and the others on his left. Those who saw the face of Jesus in the people who were the most poor and vulnerable and reached out to them with love will see the face of God in Heaven. Those who turned their backs on those in need will not.

We have Jesus' promise that if we put our faith in him, after we die, we too will be raised from the dead. Jesus' Resurrection is a promise to us. If we have faith in Jesus Christ and live a life pleasing to God, we too shall be resurrected into eternal life.

Reflection

The story of Jesus' suffering and death is also a story of love. Consider some religious and nonreligious songs you know about love. Choose some lyrics that best capture something of the love Jesus expresses for us. Write these down and explain why you have chosen them.

Bible Passages About Jesus' Death and Resurrection

Matthew 27:33–38, Mark 15:37–41, Luke 23:33–38, John 19:18–27
Jesus is crucified.

Matthew 27:45–50, Mark 15:37–41, Luke 23:44–46, John 19:28–37
Jesus dies.

Matthew 27:57–66, Mark 15:42–47, Luke 23:50–56, John 19:38–42
Jesus is buried.

Matthew 28:1–10, Mark 16:1–10, Luke 24:1–12, John 20:1–10
The Resurrection takes place.

Mark 16:12–13, Luke 24:13–35
Two disciples walk to Emmaus.

Mark 16:19–20, Luke 24:50–52, Acts 1:6–11
Jesus is taken up to Heaven.

John 20:11–18
Jesus appears to Mary Magdalene.

John 20:24–29
Jesus appears to Thomas.

JESUS' DEATH AND RESURRECTION

The story of Jesus' death and Resurrection is the center of our faith. It is told in all four Gospels. The crossword below will help you review the facts in the stories; to help you complete it, specific passages are given in parentheses after each clue.

ACROSS

2. Jesus appeared to two disciples traveling to this village. (Luke 24:13–16)
6. After Jesus ascended into heaven, two men told the Apostles that Jesus would _____. (Acts 1:11)
8. When Jesus died, the army officer, a centurion, realized that Jesus was the _____ of God. (Mark 15:39)
9. They divided Jesus' clothes among them-selves. (John 19:23)
10. Jesus asked Peter to take care of "my _____." (John 21:16)
12. He ran to the tomb when he heard that Jesus had risen. (Luke 24:10–12)
16 Mary Magdalene mistook the risen Jesus for a _____. (John 20:14–18)
17. He said he would not believe Jesus was raised unless he could touch Jesus' wounds. (John 20:24–25)
18. Some disciples recognized Jesus when he blessed and broke _____ with them. (Luke 24:30–31)
19. They had followed him from Galilee and were present at his death. (Luke 23:49)

DOWN

1. Jesus asked the Father to _____ the men who crucified him. (Luke 23:34)
3. Jesus' mother, who was present at his Crucifixion. (John 19:25–26)
4. This was rolled away from the entrance to the tomb. (Luke 24:2)
5. Jesus was crucified at Golgotha, which means "Place of the _____." (Matthew 27:33)
7. Hour of the day during which Jesus died. (Mark 15:34–37)
9. At Jesus' Ascension, he promised his followers that they would receive the Holy _____. (Acts 1:8)
11. As Jesus blessed his disciples he was taken up into _____. (Luke 24:50–52)
13. Jesus appeared to his disciples, and said, "_____ be with you." (Luke 24:36)
14. Joseph of Arimathea provided this for Jesus' body. (Mark 15:46)
15. Blood and _____ flowed out of Jesus' pierced side. (John 19:34)

Peter and his brother Andrew are fishermen working along the shores of the Sea of Galilee. Jesus calls them to leave their fishing nets and follow him. Along with ten other men, they become the first followers of Jesus. They are known as the twelve Apostles.

During Jesus' ministry, Peter and the Apostles stay with Jesus. They listen to him preach, watch him perform miracles, and grow in their faith. Jesus asks the Apostles who they think he is. Peter bravely replies that Jesus is the Messiah, the Savior that God promised.

Jesus responds to Peter's faith-filled words by saying Peter will be the foundation on which Jesus will build his Church. Symbolically, he entrusts the keys of the Church to Peter.

Peter is a man of great faith. He is also a human being with human weaknesses. Peter calls Jesus the Messiah. But when Jesus is arrested and faces death, Peter's faith is greatly shaken. Overcome by fear, Peter denies three times that he even knows Jesus. Later Peter realizes what he has done. Then he weeps in deep sorrow for his sin. Jesus later forgives him.

After Jesus' death, Peter becomes the leader of the early Church, just as Jesus promised. The once-frightened Peter preaches the Good News first to the Jews and then to the Gentiles. Peter, the simple fisherman, holds on to his belief in Jesus, is arrested, and eventually gives up his life for his faith.

Jesus chooses Peter to be the first leader of the Church. He is the first Pope. The Church is built upon the infallible truth that Peter and the Apostles teach. Christ continues to govern the Church through their successors: the Pope united with the bishops of the whole Church.

Reflection

Read Matthew 16:13–20. Why do you think Peter believes Jesus is the Messiah? If Jesus asked you the question "Who do you say I am?" what would you say?

Bible Passages About Peter

Matthew 16:13–23
Peter calls Jesus the Messiah.

Matthew 26:69–75
Peter denies Jesus.

John 1:35–42
Jesus calls Peter to be a disciple.

John 21:15–19
Jesus talks with Peter after the Resurrection.

Acts 2:14–42
Peter carries the message about Jesus.

Acts 10:34–48
The Gentiles receive the Holy Spirit.

PETER

Peter was one of Jesus' twelve Apostles and became the first Pope. Fill in the crossword below to learn more about Peter.

ACROSS

1. Jesus gave Peter the _____ of the Kingdom of heaven. (Matthew 16:19)
3. This being saved Peter from prison. (Acts 12:7–11)
5. Peter _____ bitterly because he denied Jesus. (Matthew 26:75)
7. Peter told Jesus that he and the others had _____ everything to follow Jesus. (Mark 10:28)
9. Peter walked on _____ until he became afraid. (Matthew 14:29)
11. Peter asked Jesus if he had to forgive this many times. (Matthew 18:21)
13. Jesus said he would build this upon Peter. (Matthew 16:18)
15. Peter cut an _____ off the high priest's slave. (John 18:10)
16. Peter ran here after he talked with Mary Magdalene. (Luke 24:12)
18. Peter said that Jesus had the words of eternal _____. (John 6:68)
21. Peter wanted to build these for Jesus, Moses, and Elijah. (Matthew 17:4)
22. Brother of Peter (Matthew 4:18)
23. Peter's given name (Matthew 4:18)

DOWN

2. Peter did this while Jesus prayed. (Matthew 26:40)
4. Peter came from here. (Matthew 4:18)
6. Jesus predicted that Peter would deny him this many times. (Matthew 26:34)
8. Jesus washed Peter's _____. (John 13:6–14)
10. Jesus called Peter this. (Matthew 16:18)
11. Jesus asked Peter to feed, or take care of, his _____. (John 21:17)
12. Peter used this in his occupation as a fisherman. (Matthew 4:18)
14. Peter ___ his voice loudly and spoke to the crowd. (Acts 2:14)
17. Peter answered Jesus, "You are the _____." (Mark 8:29)
19. He had Peter arrested. (Acts 12:3)
20. Jesus healed Peter's mother-___-___. (Matthew 8:14)

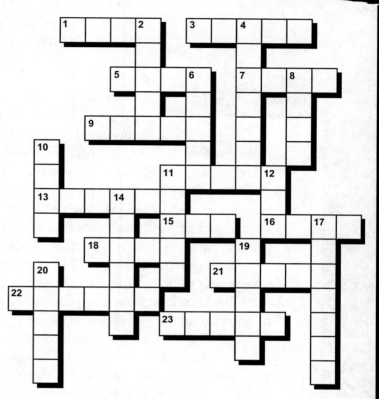

When Mary Magdalene meets Jesus, she has a troubled past. With great compassion and kindness, Jesus cures Mary Magdalene of the demons in her life. She responds by becoming part of a dedicated group of holy women who follow Jesus during his ministry. These women listen to his teachings. They use their own means to support Jesus and his Apostles as they travel around the countryside.

Following Jesus from village to village requires sacrifice, strength, and commitment. The real test of Mary Magdalene's devotion to Jesus comes when he is arrested and sentenced to be crucified. Most of Jesus' other friends abandon him during the Crucifixion. Mary Magdalene and several other women, though, stay faithfully by his cross.

After the death of Jesus, Mary Magdalene and several other women visit his tomb. They hope to give his body a proper burial according to Jewish custom. Instead of finding Jesus' dead body, they find an empty tomb. They also find an angel announcing that Jesus is not there. He has been raised!

The Gospel of John tells us Mary Magdalene is the first person to see Jesus after he rises from the dead. Mary Magdalene is weeping outside Jesus' tomb. Then Jesus appears and asks why she is crying. She does not recognize him. She thinks he is just a gardener. When Jesus calls her by name, Mary Magdalene joyfully realizes it is Jesus. He has risen from the dead.

Then Jesus sends her to tell the Apostles the Good News of his Resurrection. He wants them to share the joy of faith renewed. Because of this special mission, Christians in the early Church called Mary Magdalene the "Apostle to the Apostles." Today, Mary Magdalene remains a model of unswerving faith in Jesus and in God's plan for salvation.

Reflection

Mary Magdalene stands at the foot of Jesus' cross (see Matthew 27:45–56). She courageously risks sharing the ridicule other people give Jesus. Do you know anyone who would stand by a friend no matter what? Do you have that kind of courage?

Bible Passages About Mary Magdalene

Matthew 27:45–56, Mark 15:33–41, John 19:16–30
Mary Magdalene is present at the death of Jesus.

Matthew 27:57–61, Mark 15:42–47
Mary Magdalene is present at the burial of Jesus.

Matthew 28:1–10, Mark 16:1–8, Luke 24:1–12, John 20:1–10
Mary Magdalene visits the tomb of Jesus.

Mark 16:9–11, John 20:11–18
Jesus appears to Mary Magdalene.

Luke 8:1–3
Women accompany Jesus as he preaches.

MARY MAGDALENE

Mary Magdalene was healed by Jesus early in his ministry. She became an important leader among Jesus' disciples. Mary Magdalene is frequently mentioned in the Gospel stories about Jesus' death and Resurrection. Read the passages indicated at the end of the statements and complete this activity by filling in the answers to the clues.

1.   M __ __ __ __ __

2.   __ __ __ __ A __ __ __

3.   G __ __ __ __ __ __ __

4.   __ __ __ D __ __ __

5.   A __ __ __ __ __ __ __

6.   __ __ __ __ L __

7.   __ __ __ __ E __

8.   __ __ __ N __

9.   __ E __ __ __

1. When Jesus was crucified, Mary Magdalene stood near his cross, beside Jesus' _____. (John 19:25)

2. Jesus _____ first to Mary Magdalene after his Resurrection. (Mark 16:9)

3. Mary Magdalene thought the risen Jesus was the _____ when she first saw him. (John 20:14–16)

4. Mary Magdalene announced to the Apostles that she had seen the _____. (John 20:18)

5. Mary Magdalene went to the _____ first, to tell them what she had seen at the tomb. (Luke 24:8–10)

6. Mary Magdalene saw two _____ at the tomb of Jesus. (John 20:11–13)

7. When the Sabbath was over, Mary Magdalene and other women brought _____ to anoint Jesus' body. (Mark 16:1)

8. When Mary Magdalene went to the tomb, there was an earthquake and an angel rolled back the _____ and sat on it. (Matthew 28:1–2)

9. Jesus had driven out _____ demons from Mary Magdalene. (Mark 16:9)

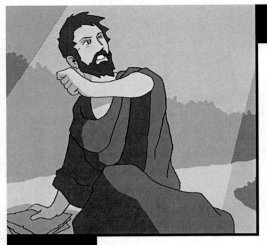

God selects many unlikely men and women to help carry out his plan for salvation. None is a more surprising choice than Paul of Tarsus.

After the death and Resurrection of Jesus, the earliest Christians are Jews who come to believe Jesus is the Messiah. This causes a great religious conflict. Many Jewish leaders insist people are saved from sin by following the Jewish Law. Christians believe people are saved from sin by following Jesus.

As a Jewish leader, Paul is committed to stopping the spread of Christian ideas. He is willing to do anything to reach his goals. He will even imprison Christians and allow them to be killed.

Paul travels to the city of Damascus in Syria to persecute Christians. On the road Paul has a life-changing encounter with the risen Christ. The experience is so powerful that Paul asks to be baptized. Then he begins preaching to others that Jesus is the Messiah. The dramatic event and his conversion, or change of heart, to Christianity influence Paul for the rest of his life. The one-time enemy of the Church becomes the Church's best-known missionary. He takes long and dangerous journeys all over the Roman Empire to spread Jesus' teachings.

When he arrives in a new town, Paul first preaches in the Jewish synagogue. Sometimes the Jews reject him. Then he preaches to the Gentiles, or non-Jews. They often welcome his message. Paul clearly understands that the Gospel message is for all people, Jews and Gentiles alike. He teaches that faith in Jesus, not the Jewish Law, is the only way to salvation.

A heroic saint, Paul endures many trials and hardships in order to preach the Gospel. Much of what Paul teaches is found in the New Testament letters he writes to the Christian communities he visits. Those writings help unite our faith today to that of the earliest Christians.

Reflection

Read Acts 9:1–19. It tells the story of Paul's conversion. Paul's experience is a dramatic "wow!" moment. Anyone can have an experience of Jesus and see the world differently because of it. Have you ever had a wow experience of God? Have you ever had an experience that helped you see someone in your life in a new way? How did that happen?

Bible Passages About Paul

Acts 9:1–19
Paul is converted.

Acts 16:16–40
Paul and Silas are miraculously freed from jail.

Romans 8:31–39
God loves us in Christ Jesus.

1 Corinthians 12:12–31
Christ is one body, many parts.

2 Corinthians 4:7–12
Spiritual treasures are found in clay pots.

Galatians 2:20
Christ lives in us.

PAUL

At first, Paul (whose name was also Saul) persecuted the followers of Jesus. After a dramatic conversion experience, Paul became one of the greatest missionaries for Christ.

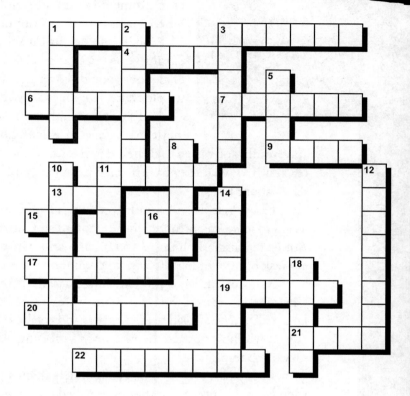

ACROSS

1. The Lord wanted Paul to go to this city. (Acts 23:11)
3. Paul was dragged out of this in Jerusalem. (Acts 21:27–30)
4. Paul was shipwrecked on this island. (Acts 28:1)
6. Saul escaped danger in this. (Acts 9:25)
7. Paul was ___ and dragged out of the city. (Acts 14:19)
9. Some Jews planned to ___ Saul. (Acts 9:23)
11. The soldier was surprised to know that Paul could speak this. (Acts 21:37)
13. Paul was in prison twice for ___ years each time. (Acts 24:27; 28:30)
15. Saul heard a voice that said, "Why do you persecute ___?" (Acts 22:7)
16. The ___ priest made charges against Paul (Acts 24:1)
17. Saul was trying to destroy this. (Acts 8:3)
19. Paul was upset because of the number of these in Athens. (Acts 17:16)
20. He baptized Saul. (Acts 9:17–19)
21. Paul preached the good ___ in many places. (Acts 14:21)
22. Paul converted Jews and ___. (Acts 14:1–2)

DOWN

1. Paul was a ___ citizen. (Acts 16:37; 22:27)
2. Paul wanted this man to decide his case. (Acts 25:21)
3. Saul was from this city. (Acts 9:11)
5. The Holy Spirit had ___ for Saul to do. (Acts 13:2)
8. Paul went to see this governor. (Acts (23:24)
10. Saul was present at his stoning. (Acts 7:58–60)
11. The people in Lystra thought Paul was a ___. (Acts 14:11–12)
12. He helped Saul. (Acts 9:27)
14. Paul was a member of this Jewish group. (Acts 23:6)
18. Saul's condition after he was knocked to the ground. (Acts 9:3–9)

Priscilla and her husband, Aquila, are a Jewish couple. They live in Rome. They stay there until an order from the emperor forces all Jewish residents to leave the city. From Rome Priscilla and Aquila move to the city of Corinth. It becomes one of the most important moves of their lives.

Priscilla and Aquila earn their living as tent makers. In Corinth they meet and befriend another tent maker, named Paul. They soon discover that Paul is much more than a simple craftsman. He is also a dedicated follower of Jesus.

Paul shares his faith with Priscilla and Aquila. Over time they too became Christians. Following Paul's example Priscilla and Aquila don't keep their newfound faith to themselves. Enthusiastically they teach others what they have learned from Paul and have come to believe for themselves about Jesus.

Later Priscilla and Aquila travel with Paul to the city of Ephesus. Paul soon leaves to make many more journeys to spread Christian teachings. Priscilla and Aquila remain in Ephesus. As a husband-and-wife team, they take up the missionary task of developing a Christian community there.

Many of our large, modern congregations gather in huge buildings. Early Christian groups, on the other hand, were so small they often met in private homes. There they read the Scriptures and celebrated the Eucharist. Priscilla and Aquila willingly opened their home as a meeting place for the small faith community of Ephesus.

In one of his last letters, Paul publicly thanks Priscilla and Aquila for their friendship. He notes that they even risked their lives for him. Paul recognizes them for all the work they have done in sharing the Good News of Jesus Christ with those who did not yet believe. We remember Priscilla and Aquila today as a missionary couple. They took their faith seriously and worked to share God's word with others.

Reflection

Priscilla and Aquila help the early church grow by welcoming people into their home to pray. When do you feel most welcome in other people's homes? How do you make other people feel welcome in your home?

Bible Passages About Priscilla and Aquila

Acts 18:1–4
Paul meets Priscilla and Aquila in Corinth.

Acts 18:18–20
Priscilla and Aquila travel to Ephesus with Paul.

Acts 18:24–26
Priscilla and Aquila teach Apollos.

Romans 16:3–5
Paul greets Priscilla, Aquila, and their community.

1 Corinthians 16:19
Paul sends Priscilla's and Aquila's greetings.

2 Timothy 4:19
Timothy is asked to greet Priscilla and Aquila.

PRISCILLA AND AQUILA

Priscilla and Aquila were dedicated Christians of the first century. Most of their story is in Acts, chapter 18, but they are also mentioned in Romans 16:3–4, 1 Corinthians 16:19, and 2 Timothy 4:19. Read these passages and complete the following statements about Priscilla and Aquila. To find out if your answers are correct, check for each of your answers in the word search. Put the unused letters from the word search in the spaces at the bottom of the page to spell out a fact about Priscilla and Aquila.

1. Priscilla and Aquila were originally from __ __ __ __ __.

2. They left Rome because the Emperor __ __ __ __ __ __ __ __ ordered all the Jews to leave.

3. They moved to __ __ __ __ __ __ __.

4. There they met __ __ __ __.

5. He stayed with them and worked with them because they were all __ __ __ __   __ __ __ __ __ __ by trade.

6. They sailed together to __ __ __ __ __.

7. Priscilla and Aquila then lived in __ __ __ __ __ __ __ __.

8. They met a man named __ __ __ __ __ __ __.

9. He was well versed in the Scriptures and knew about Jesus, but Priscilla and Aquila instructed him in the __ __ __   __ __   __ __ __.

10. Priscilla and Aquila risked their __ __ __ __ __ for Paul.

11. A church met in their __ __ __ __ __.

C	P	T	S	R	A	I	S	L	C	W
O	I	E	L	U	L	I	I	A	A	A
R	N	N	P	D	I	V	R	Y	A	A
I	Q	T	U	H	E	D	O	Y	P	I
N	L	M	A	S	E	F	U	O	S	P
T	W	A	E	R	G	S	L	A	A	E
H	W	K	O	O	H	L	U	U	L	R
K	E	E	D	O	O	R	L	S	S	C
I	N	R	U	S	I	T	A	L	Y	T
H	E	S	S	E	R	V	I	C	E	O
F	E	J	E	S	U	S	+	+	+	+

__ __ __ __ __ __ __ __ __ __ __ __   __ __ __

__ __ __ __ __ __ __ __ __   __ __ __ __ __

__ __ __ __ __ __ __ __ __ __ __ __

__ __ __ __ __ __ __ __ __ __ __

__ __   __ __ __ __ __ __ __.

(Romans 16:3)